MW00484245

Ms. Jean L. Dilsaver
3662 SW 20th St.
Okeechobee, FL 34974

THE ADMINISTRATOR'S GUIDE
TO
PERSONAL PRODUCTIVITY
with the
Time Management Checklist

by
Harold L. Taylor

For information about permission to reproduce selections from this book, writ
Eye On Education, Permissions Dept., Box 388, Princeton Junction, N.J. 08550

LIBRARY OF CONGRESS CATALOG CARD NUMBER: 93-70823

ISBN 1-883001-01-3

Printed in the United States of America

Printing 9 8 7 6 5 4 3 2 1

About the Author

Harold Taylor spent 18 years in teaching, administration and business before forming Harold Taylor Time Consultants Inc. with offices in St. Petersburg, Florida and Toronto, Canada. He is the author of nine books, over 100 articles, a monthly newsletter, and a video training program, all in the area of time management. Creator of the "Taylor Time Planner" and other time management aids, he conducts seminars and workshops throughout North America on personal organization and time and life management.

Acknowledgements

I would like to thank the following educators for their useful advice and editorial input during the preparation of this manuscript. Their attention to detail is sincerely appreciated:

John O'Mahoney, Principal
Southampton Intermediate School
Southampton, NY

E. Bruce Meeks, Associate Professor
Department of Educational Administration
University of North Texas
Denton, TX

I would also like to thank the following people who participated in the focus group which helped draw our attention to the need for this book and helped shape its direction and goals:

Joseph Anzek, Principal
Brunswick Acres School
Kendall Park, NJ

Marjorie Castro, Principal
Dobbs Ferry Middle School
Dobbs Ferry, NY

Thomas Fazio, Principal
Hastings High School
Hastings-on-Hudson, NY

Carol Kleban, Principal
Professional Children's School
New York, NY

Daniel Woodard, Assistant Principal
White Plains High School
White Plains, NY

Finally, a sincere thank you to Joan Patterson for her assistance in preparing the manuscript, and publisher Bob Sickles for his encouragement and enthusiasm for this project.

Contents

Can we really manage time? How overtime
extends inefficiency. Savoring gifts of time. The
hidden costs of time savers. Why organizers
won't get you organized. The key to personal
productivity.

The difference between goals and purpose.
Determining your mission in life. The importance
of having a professional mission statement. How
to develop a personal mission statement to direct
your future.

Why goals are necessary in an administrator's
personal as well as professional life.
Characteristics of workable goals. Making your
goals achievable.

List of Exhibits

Introduction

School administrators are charged with an awesome responsibility—helping fashion the future of the United States. The time demands are also awesome—teacher evaluations, meetings, observations, conferences, paperwork, telephone calls, and a myriad of other activities consuming time. Research indicates that the school principal is the key to the level and quality of education within the school. From superintendents to assistant principals, the onus is upon administrators to be leaders, managers, counselors, encouragers, change agents and achievers. They are to be both effective and efficient, doing what is necessary and doing it well. Managers of time.

And yet you cannot manage time, you can only manage yourself. You don't keep a tidy desk in order to get organized; you keep a tidy desk because you *are* organized.

All the theory in the world won't prevent a crisis from occurring. Neither can you eliminate meetings, interruptions, telephone calls, drop-in visitors, even though they are cited as major time problems. Personal organizers, planners, time-saving gadgets will not get you organized any more than working long hours will make you effective.

What you have to do is take charge of your own life. You

cannot manage time, but you can manage yourself with respect to the time that you do have. And although organizers and planners won't get you organized, you can use these time management tools properly so the process will be a little easier.

And it is a process. You cannot become organized by reading a book or attending a seminar—only by putting the suggestions into practice over an extended period of time. We are creatures of habit. Since it took years to form ineffective habits, it will also take years to replace them with effective ones.

Getting organized and increasing your personal productivity is a lifelong process. But you will experience improvements and reap rewards within a few weeks if you take action on many of the ideas suggested in this book.

Be patient. Don't attempt too much at once. And don't give up on something just because it doesn't work right away. It takes weeks to form a new habit.

At the back of this book there is a time management checklist for those who have immediate problems in specific areas. These are merely band-aids; they will not get you organized. But they may get you out of some immediate trouble. These ideas were collected from my previous nine books, seminars and articles, as well as from other peoples' experiences. If you don't have time to read this book, put a dozen or so of the best ideas into action right away. Then use the time that you save to read this book.

Harold Taylor
Toronto, Ontario
March 15, 1993

Chapter 1

Is Time Management A Myth?

EXTENDING YOUR INEFFICIENCY

Managing time does not mean working longer hours. Many successful and wealthy people credit their success to their long hours of dedication to the job. Aristotle Onassis, the multi-millionaire business tycoon, was quoted as saying "I have learned the value and importance of time; therefore, I work two additional hours each day and in that way I gain the equivalent of one additional month each year."

There is no doubt that longer hours will provide additional results proportionate to the results you obtain during your normal working hours. But if you are only 50% effective during the day, you will be only 50% effective during your *extended* day as well. Are you willing to sacrifice 4 hours of your personal time to obtain 2 hours of professional results?

It would make more sense to maximize your effectiveness during regular working hours, eliminating the time wasters and using the time saved to work on priorities. Effectiveness involves working on priorities. A principal spending time with a teacher, for example, resulting in improved teaching, could influence a generation of students. And a superintendent, devoting time each day to achieving a professional goal, could have a positive impact on everyone within his or her area of influence. Effective administrators recognize that it's more important to utilize their time wisely than to attempt to get more time to utilize. It is not wise to *extend* inefficiencies. You must *eliminate* them.

Once you become extremely effective during the day, with minimal wasted time, you can extend this effective time into the evenings. That is, if you want to become an Aristotle Onassis. Most of us will settle for a successful career and a successful home life. You may not even want to aim for the top—you will pass many workaholics enroute.

How many hours you work is up to you. We all have different personal objectives. But from a time management standpoint it is unwise to extend your working hours *until* you are managing your present working hours as effectively and efficiently as possible.

SAVOR THOSE GIFTS OF TIME

It is estimated that the average person wastes nine years of his or her life standing in line, opening junk mail, waiting for red lights and trying to reach people on the telephone. It's those little meaningless activities that become so meaningful over an extended period of time. Time does add up. The frustrating thing about it is that you can't get too much accomplished while waiting for a red light to change or for the clerk at the checkout desk to wait on you. The time is lost before you realize it's there to be used.

It's okay to resolve to bring a book with you to read while in lineups, or balance your checkbook while waiting at the hairdressers, or listen to a 3-minute segment of a motivational tape while brushing your teeth. But how practical is all of this? Unless you buckle on a holster every morning with pockets for books, cassette player, magazines, checkbooks, tapes and sundry one-minute tasks, you are rarely prepared for action when the brief delay does occur. And even then, you had better be fast on the draw, because you have to complete that one-minute task before you become a bottleneck yourself.

The point is that the major portion of this lost time will never be redeemed, and we have to accept that fact without becoming paranoid. That is not to say that being prepared to utilize idle time for filler jobs is not a good idea. Lord knows I've emphasized that strategy along with hundreds of other well-meaning time management "experts" for years. But it's about time the pendulum took a backward swing before we lose sight of reality. The reality is that sometimes utilizing segments of idle time is not possible, frequently it's not practical, and always it's not essential. For all we know, God has allocated to us four score years and ten, the ten being an allowance for unavoidable delays.

When we become obsessed with the productive utilization of time, our quality of life suffers. We are upset by momentary delays, angered by red lights or slow vehicles, and absolutely livid if someone beats us to a parking space, necessitating another tour of the lot. We tend to compensate for these unavoidable delays by putting the rest of our life on fast-forward. We run up "up" escalators, share the same segment of a revolving door, push an elevator button, then use the stairs. We buy lunch in a fast-food outlet and eat it while we drive, microwave our dinner and have simultaneous "quality" time with our family and the TV set.

Our professional life is no less hectic. Plagued by interruptions, unrealistic deadlines, incessant telephone messages and a flow of paperwork that appears to be spring fed, we are urged to increase our productivity through books, seminars, videos, cassettes on the efficient management of time. Well and good. But the emphasis in those time management programs should not be on how to utilize those fragments of idle time that consume nine years of our life. Frequently those "time wasters" are the only relief we get. They help us to survive during the remaining four score years.

What we *should* be learning is how to eliminate low payback activities, delegate, plan, prioritize, schedule, avoid stress— and above all else—how *not* to feel guilty about squandering those precious minutes while driving, waiting, or dispensing with junk mail. Those "wasted" minutes may be the very thing that keeps *us* from being wasted—if we can learn to accept them as physical, mental and emotional breaks, and not feel compelled to fill them with more frantic activity. A minute or two of relaxation, deep breathing, shoulder hunching, or mind soothing daydreaming may be just what the doctor ordered. Not being able to slip our body and mind into idle when a delay occurs could be dangerous to our health. The compulsion to remain busy could have us switching from one line to another in a fruitless effort to get waited on first. Or we could find ourselves risking lives by racing through an orange light in order to wait longer at the next one. Or we could miss our bus stop in an attempt to finish one more paragraph of that book that didn't need reading—necessitating the purchase of another book for the long trip back. Imagine the feelings of frustration, the anger, the stress caused by such situations and it's not difficult to believe that everyday hassles such as these are more physically damaging than all the major life crises we are likely to encounter.

Most of us think we manage our time quite well. But have we lost the ability to relax in the process? Let's allow ourselves some quality time with our thoughts. It's during those idle moments when we are at our creative best. Buried experiences have a chance to resurface. Ideas spring into our conscious mind. We have time to reflect on past accomplishments and future pursuits. We are able to put life in perspective and ponder our future. The alternative is to keep ourselves so preoccupied with minor tasks that we don't realize we're not getting anywhere.

Sure, it's okay to read a report during that flight to a workshop or conference, rehearse your presentation on that long drive to the school, and listen to inspirational tapes as you drive to an out-of-town conference. It's usually a good idea to make productive use of extended periods of time that are not needed for personal renewal. But don't feel obliged to cram a one minute task into every 30-second delay that occurs. Instead, look upon that unpredictable delay as a gift of time to be "wasted" at will. Seldom will this brief respite actually be a waste. It will be an island of time in a turbulent sea of activity.

TIME SAVERS HAVE A HIDDEN COST

Modern technology is supposed to make life easier for us by relieving us of the routine so we can concentrate on those priority tasks that lead to the achievement of our goals. But it seems to me that the cellular phone, beepers, laptop computers and sundry miniaturized gadgetry are being aimed at increasing our efficiency through the utilization of otherwise "idle" time. Excessive driving time, essential travel, inevitable periods of waiting, could all be made productive through the use of these high-tech wonders.

But are we becoming enslaved by the very things we have created? No longer are we content to utilize idle time. These "time savers" are infringing on the relaxation time we need so badly. We listen to educational tapes while we jog, talk on the telephone while we dine out, and view business videos on 8mm portable playback machines by the pool.

We are becoming fanatics—to the extent that legislation may have to be passed to protect us from ourselves. Already, patrons of movie theaters in the U.S. are being asked to check their cellular phones at the door. Restaurants and other businesses are beginning to ban portable phones as customers complain about the noise. My wife and I watched in dismay a few months ago as a man walked into a restaurant with a young lady on his arm and a cellular phone on his ear. Although the lady left his arm as they were seated, the phone never left his ear. It was still there while they ordered, and still there when we left. Obviously a touching example of quality time with a loved one.

There's nothing wrong with increasing efficiency during working hours. But increasing efficiency while crowding out personal time, relaxation and recreational time is ineffective and unhealthy. Our lives become unbalanced, and efficiency becomes the goal rather than simply a means of achieving a goal. We soon lose sight of our purpose in life. We sacrifice meaning for means.

Time saving devices are great. But beware—the life they shorten may be your own. They all have their hidden costs. Just as most of us would like to retain our friends, even though they consume much of our time, so we would also like to retain some of our activities in their present form, even though they could be streamlined by technology.

The point is, moving sidewalks and high-speed escalators may get us from point A to point B a lot faster. But it's not to our benefit if we enjoyed the walk. As composer Hector Berlioz is quoted as having said, "Time is the great teacher, but unfortunately it kills all of its students." So why not enjoy what time has to offer instead of hurrying it along to its conclusion.

Before we adopt any time saving suggestion or purchase any time saving gadget, we should ask ourselves the cost. Not only the financial outlay, but the cost to our quality of life. Otherwise, we may be deceived into sacrificing a piece of ourselves in the name of efficiency.

What is a benefit-laden time saver to one person may be an infringement on personal dignity to another. Don't assume that all time saving methods, techniques or ideas should be universal. Typing is faster than longhand writing, but does a typed letter from Mother have the same warmth? A fax is faster than the mail, but is something lost when you no longer have to rip open one of those infrequent letters from your son in college? Perhaps some of us like going out to the theater or cooking an "old fashioned" meal, or, heaven forbid, holding a personal meeting with real people instead of a series of TV monitors.

This is not a reversal of opinion on the wisdom of time management strategies. It is to caution those who would move too quickly to adopt a time saver without first evaluating its long-term (and short-term) impact on the school or on the personal lives of the teachers, staff and students. And to suggest that what appears to be a time saver to some might be perceived as a threat to others.

AN ORGANIZER WON'T GET YOU ORGANIZED

If high-tech time savers utilizing every minute of the day, or working longer hours are not the keys to personal productivity, what is? Many would have us believe it's the personal organizers, those multi-ringed, multi-sectioned binders in which we maintain everything from our telephone conversations to our kid's clothing sizes.

According to Lucy Hedrick, author of *Five Days To An Organized Life* (Dell Publishing, 1990), there are at present over 300 organizers or personal planning aids on the market, with sales expected to exceed $200 million. Add to that the hundreds of books, videos, cassettes and seminars on time management available, and you would think we would be the most organized individuals who ever walked planet Earth.

Truth is, millions of people feel overloaded, over stressed and overwhelmed by the demands on their time. "Not enough time" is still the number one complaint of education's leaders.

Why this apparent dichotomy? Time remains untouched by the thousands of timesaving gimmicks lying unused on desktops, bottom drawers and briefcases. No organizer devised will ever effect the amount of time at our disposal. God alone has that power. And though faith in God is justified, only fools put their faith in organizers.

This is not to say that organizers are useless. They are good time management tools if you use them properly. The problem is that people seem to lack the self-discipline to make them work. The place to start is with ourselves—time management from the inside out, if you will. By replacing inefficient habits such as making mental notes, interrupting ourselves and others needlessly, not listening, shuffling papers, etc., with efficient habits such as making notes in an organized manner while on the telephone, and jotting down those thoughts for later action instead of interrupting others, we can more fully utilize the time at our disposal.

Organizers and other time management aids can be used effectively during the process of forming new habits. But the organizers do none of the changing. The changing is entirely up to ourselves. If we manage *ourselves*, we are managing our time.

THE KEY TO PERSONAL PRODUCTIVITY

Some people shrug off their disorganization by claiming they were born that way. Others claim they are so organized they were born on their due dates. But personal organization is not hereditary. You acquire your habits, good or bad, as you grow older. The more bad habits you have acquired, the more difficult it is to get organized; but it *can* be done.

That's the good news. The bad news is it takes effort. Nothing worthwhile comes easily. Anyone can resolve to get up a half hour earlier, for example; but actually getting up requires effort. It takes varying degrees of effort putting things back after using them, purging the files, developing the "do it now" habit, and tearing yourself away from pleasant but unproductive tasks.

So you must want to get organized badly enough to endure some temporary unpleasantness. You must be self-motivated. No seminar, book, or newsletter is ever going to give you the incentive to persist in your efforts to get organized. That's a fact that you must accept.

So where does the motivation come from? Motivation is a product of the amount of desire to get organized multiplied by the expectancy that you will succeed. If you are experiencing few problems the way you are, and are happy with the results you are achieving, you will have a low desire to change. But if you are convinced that you can get more accomplished and lead a better life if you were more time-effective, your desire will be high. It only remains for you to be convinced that certain changes *will* lead to personal organization.

Confirmation of is available from other individuals, as well as myself, who have succeeded in changing habits and increasing their effectiveness. So read the books on goal-setting, success and time management authored by individuals who *did* succeed using their own methods. There are plenty of testimonials that goal-setting, planning, self-discipline and persistence pay off. If you believe it, and you want it for yourself, you will *have* the motivation.

To assist in this belief, I will review in the following chapters some guidelines for managing yourself effectively with respect to time. You will never be able to manage time itself; it's already as organized as it will ever get. Noon comes at the same time every day; two o'clock always follows one o'clock. It's like clockwork. (It *is* clockwork!) Time management is a myth. But personal organization is something you *can* achieve.

Instead of wasting time attempting to eliminate all the time wasters, concentrate on the 80% of your activities where real inroads into productivity gains are possible. Establishing your purpose in life, setting goals, planning and prioritizing, scheduling, and accomplishing those meaningful tasks—here is where the real value lies.

If someone threw $11,100 onto the ground, consisting of an equal number of bills of $1, $10, and $100 denominations, and told you to keep whatever you could gather in one minute, which ones would you go after? You could grab a lot more bills if you simply grabbed whatever you encountered first. And no doubt, those $1 bills do add up. But I dare say if you ignored the small ones and went after all those big $100 bills, you would be a lot richer one minute later.

Strange as it may seem, many people go through life grabbing at every opportunity that comes along without really having a plan to fish where the big fish are. And busily stuffing $1 and $10 bills into their pockets, their time runs out before they achieve anything of significance.

To ensure that you are focusing on the significant activities, develop a personal and professional mission statement (or review the ones you have already developed), set goals compatible with your mission, and schedule those goal-related activities into your planner. The next few chapters will show you how.

Chapter 2

Developing A Mission Statement

GOALS VS. PURPOSE

In general, people are good at maximizing their career potential; but few are good at maximizing their life potential. Focusing too intently on time management at work while ignoring others could cause one to win at work and lose in life. Viewing time management as *life* management forces us to apply time management skills to all areas, including family, leisure, finances, church, volunteer involvements and self-development.

Whereas time management usually starts with goal-setting, life management starts with the development of a personal mission statement or the determination of your purpose in life. Unlike goals, a purpose is seldom measurable and never fully attainable during your lifetime. Rather, it is your *reason for living*. It is your motivation to get up in the morning and endure hardships, overcome adversities, persist through setbacks, and maintain enthusiasm into the golden years.

Most people do not consciously think about their purpose in life, let alone reduce it to writing in the form of a personal mission statement. Others view their goals as their purpose for living and upon reaching their goals lose their reason for living. This is particularly evident when people concentrate on the achievement of professional goals to the exclusion of other areas of their lives. Upon retirement, they drift without purpose and die prematurely. Psychologist Abraham Maslow claimed that the quality and quantity of a person's life varied directly with his or her sense of purpose at mid-life. Without a reason for living, people simply don't live.

Activities should be derived from your purpose, not the reverse. And yet many people, convinced that happiness and fulfilment depends upon setting and achieving goals within a work environment, become so engrossed in their profession that work *becomes* their reason for living. Their status, friendships, self-esteem and identity are all connected with their position at work. When that connection is severed, their life collapses.

Ironically, the things that most people count as important in their lives are not the things they are remembered for—if they are remembered at all. Bob Shank, author of *Total Life Management* (Multnomah Press, 1990), uses an interesting exercise in his seminars. He asks people to jot down the names of the greatest people in history (*e.g.*, Joan of Arc, Thomas Edison, Albert Einstein), then to note the one thing that distinguishes them as great. Seldom do these things relate to their material possessions, incomes, hobbies, travels or recreational preferences. Most of them had a single-minded purpose to which they dedicated their lives. To quote Shank: "The great men and women of history were not great because of what they owned or earned, but rather for what they gave their lives to accomplish."

Once you have established a personal mission statement, your goals and activities will reflect the values expressed in this mission statement.

FINDING YOUR MISSION IN LIFE

What is your purpose in life? Why do you exist? In order to make your time on earth meaningful, fulfilling and rewarding, you should be doing the kinds of things that reflect your purpose or mission. Educator Vic Conant of Nightingale-Conant was quoted as saying: "I think that I can consider myself as successful if I am able to look upon everyone with love. In life you are either serving a purpose, or you are just serving time. I really want to spend the majority of my time in service to other people." Vic Conant had a mission. Consultant Naomi Rhode, was introduced at a conference as a person whose purpose was "to elicit growth and change in the lives of those who hear her." Naomi Rhode has a mission.

A purpose is what motivates us to action, to commitment, and to success. Without a mission, goals are meaningless and results are unfulfilling.

William James claimed that the most important thing in life is to live your life for something more important than your life. Your life purpose describes the focus of your life and sets the stage for goal-setting and time management.

Although most people have some vague awareness of their purpose in life, they have never taken the effort to reflect on it, and put it into writing. Once expressed on paper, it can become a guide for setting goals and scheduling activities. It prevents you from setting goals inconsistent with your purpose—a common cause of dissatisfaction and stress. It also becomes the source of your motivation and provides the "reason for living" expressed earlier. It ensures that your life has a consistent direction and inherent value. You know that what you are doing is worthwhile and deserving of effort. Your self-esteem is enhanced and decision-making becomes easier. And finally, you will be a success—as long as your life coincides with your purpose.

If you have trouble expressing your personal mission statement, ask others for theirs and compare them with your own values. Or hear what others are saying about you. Stephanie Culp's example from her book, *Streamlining Your Life*: "My mission in life is to be loving and generous to my friends and family and those in need, and to provide a moral guidepost for my children to live by and emulate."

Since personal mission statements are "personal," it's impossible to judge whether someone's stated purpose is right or wrong, or whether it is complete, too long or too short. Mission statements could encompass several pages or a few words, but most people subscribe to a brief statement of purpose. Author Roger Merrill suggests that it contain three things: What you want to be, what you want to do or accomplish, and the values and principles upon which your being and doing are based. Author Sybil Stanton suggests that your purpose or mission be a statement of what you give to life regardless of what life gives to you. Goals can change, but a mission or purpose remains constant.

WRITE DOWN YOUR MISSION

Most of the people who have a clear set of tangible personal goals, have never really taken the time to examine their mission in life. A failure to examine your values first may result in goals that are at cross-purposes to them. Discomfort, stress, and feelings of guilt may ensue. If your pursuits are in harmony with your values you will be happy—at peace with yourself.

The number of values is unlimited and will vary from person to person. Home life is a value. Doing God's will is a value. Fame is a value. Materialism, self-reliance, sincerity, freedom, career, friendship, health, morality are all values. Participate in a brain-storming activity alone or with a partner. Write down all the things that you feel are important to you. Values are things we consider worthwhile—our personal standards. They establish our sense of purpose and direction. If we fail to examine our values first, we may be working toward a goal that is at cross-purposes to them. Writing them down ensures that we are able to express them, understand them, and become committed to them. We may think we know what we want. but thoughts are fleeting; words on paper are more concrete.

Once our beliefs are on paper, we can evaluate them, change them, and make them adequately express where we stand as individuals. Keep that mission statement handy as you formulate your goals. Reconsider any goals that seem to conflict with your values. The result should be a set of goals that are consistent with your purpose in life. They will be much easier to achieve. And a lot more enjoyable.

Your personal mission is not your vocation—it *determines* your vocation. Nor is it the same as your school's mission, although it should be compatible. My personal mission, for example, is "To help others organize their lives by sharing ideas through books, seminars, and by personal example so they are free to do the work God has given them to do." It would be difficult for me to fulfil my mission by working in a factory or an office. But it could be fulfilled in an educational environment or as a consultant, speaker, or writer.

If your mission is compatible with your work, you will be more motivated, experience less stress, become more effective and find greater fulfilment in the performance of your job.

AN ORGANIZATION'S MISSION

Every school should have a mission statement that is reviewed periodically. Administrators and teachers will feel more motivated to meet daily goals once they understand the overall thrust of the organization. The most important factor in forming a team is unity of purpose. A mission statement expresses that purpose.

It will be a lot easier to communicate a mission statement to others if it is brief and simple. At most it should contain the type of organization, its philosophy, services provided and clients or communities serviced.

A mission statement or statement of purpose forces schools to identify why they are really in existence. Nightingale-Conant, for example, recognized they were in the "idea" business, not the cassette or video tape business, with their mission "to produce and distribute ideas that help improve people's lives." Similarly, railroads are in the transportation business and manufacturers of games are in the entertainment business. A school's mission statement, such as the following one from Southampton Intermediate School, provides the direction needed to set and implement goals:

"We, the Southampton Intermediate School Educational Community, are committed to establishing a true partnership among students, teachers, parents, and the entire community for the benefit of all.

Our mission is to create a positive atmosphere where learning is valued, where differences are respected, and where each student develops responsibility for continued intellectual, educational, physical, personal and social growth.

We are responsible for providing a curriculum that educates all students to their fullest potential, promotes confident youth development, and fosters mutual and self respect."

Developing a professional mission statement forces school boards and administrators to think through their plans for the future and develop a statement that will encompass those plans. Once developed, it should be reflected in any goals set by administrators. It keeps everyone on course and prevents individuals from pursuing goals which are inconsistent with the purpose of the school.

The mission statement gives birth to goals or objectives, which in turn translate into plans—culminating in action. We succeed by working together to achieve goals which reflect our purpose or mission.

Chapter 3

How To Set Goals

THE NEED FOR GOALS

Once you have examined your values and have a good idea of the direction you want to take in your career and life, it is important to draw up some specific goals for your personal life as well as your professional life. The reason is that goals:

- Create a climate for motivation.

- Enable us to plan and gain greater control over our own destinies.

- Add challenge to our lives and a sense of achievement.

- Provide a means of self-evaluation.

- Make us results-oriented so we work smarter, not harder.

- Add a new dimension of meaning to our lives.

- Enable us to manage our time more effectively.

- Reduce the stress normally attributed to the feeling of "not getting anywhere."

* Increase our chances of success.

* Allow us to determine whether our jobs are compatible with the things we really want out of life.

In spite of these advantages of goal-setting and the personal endorsements given to it by successful goal-setters, it is not widespread. According to Paul Zimmerman, president of a financial planning firm, among high income persons,

* more than half have no wills;

* many have little idea of family worth on the death of the breadwinner;

* most have inadequate tax counsel;

* less than half plan financially for their children's education;

* many don't know their own company benefits.

Few successful people will deny that there is a direct relationship between their goal-setting and their success. And since an estimated 95% of the population have no clear-cut personal goals in writing, it's understandable why so many people feel frustrated and unfulfilled.

Goal-setting is a powerful tool. There is no limit to what you can achieve, given the time and motivation to do so. Within ten years you can effect a complete career change, obtain a Ph.D. in Education, save enough money to tour Europe, achieve a superintendency—or become a millionaire or best-selling author or well-known educational consultant.

But to achieve any of these things you must (a) honestly ask yourself if you really *want* to, and (b) establish a *written* goal to that effect, along with short-term objectives that progressively lead to that goal. If you have already developed a personal mission statement, setting specific personal goals will be much easier. You have probably already considered what is important in your life and the things you would like to accomplish. If you're not sure what you want out of life and what it is you want to do or accomplish, start thinking about it right now!

DEVELOP SOME PERSONAL GOALS

To get started on this "self-analysis," jot down any of the following items that appeal to you. Add others that come to mind. Some of the items you jot down or add may become the basis of a goal in itself. Others will keep you from setting a goal that would be in conflict with those things you really enjoy in life. Here are a few examples to get you thinking:

- Having an interesting career.
- Having a happy, satisfying marriage.
- Running your own company.
- Spending time with interesting friends.
- Having a comfortable home in the suburbs, or city or country.
- Living in a modern apartment resort in the heart of an exciting city.
- Producing a great work of art or best-selling novel.
- Having enough free time and money to travel.
- Getting to really know and understand your family, and spending quality time with them.
- Staying in good physical condition.
- Having people consult with you because you are an expert in some field of education.
- Making enough money to travel, educate your children, and buy whatever luxuries you desire.
- Working in a high-level job and influencing the direction of a major school district.
- Having an interesting hobby.
- Spending time in meditation, prayer, and spiritual development.

* Retiring at the age of 55, 65 or 70.

* Changing careers or going back to school.

Can you think of any others? Conduct a brainstorming session with yourself or, better still, with your family. Write down what you really enjoy doing. What gives you a sense of satisfaction, achievement, self-esteem, personal growth? Then, from the list, select a few priorities—those things you want above everything else—and see if you can express it in terms of a goal. For example, if authoring a best-selling novel appeals to you, and you think you will feel the same way in the future, one of your goals might be "to complete a 100,000-word novel by Dec. 31, 1996, which has the *potential* to become a best-seller." (No author can actually write a bestseller; the publisher, media, and the public determine its success.)

Your shorter term objectives might include things like "complete a 10-week fiction writing course at Florida State by June 15;" "read six bestsellers currently on the market by November 15, 1996;" and so on. Your goals and objectives should be well thought out and reduced to writing. They must be realistic, measurable, and compatible with each another and with your desired lifestyle. You must have the self-discipline to pursue each short-term goal relentlessly, focusing on the rewards of the eventual achievement and not on the temporary discomfort of the pursuit.

A seminar trainer once suggested that if you keep participants busy enough, they won't realize they're not learning anything. The same thing applies to life; if you keep yourself busy enough, rushing from job to job, you won't realize you're not *getting* anywhere.

It's important to stop from time to time and take inventory. One thing's certain. If you find you *do* want to achieve something, chances are you *can* do it—if your desire to succeed is strong enough. It has often been pointed out that we tend to become precisely what we imagine ourselves to be. All that we need are concrete goals and a step-by-step plan of action. So, don't *wait* for opportunities, make your own. If you want to get something in the *future*, the time to start is *now*, in the *present*. Don't be afraid to put your ambitions in writing. And don't be discouraged by the fact that your goals may not be reached for another five or more years. It's better to aim for success in the long run than never know what success feels like.

THE EXTRAPOLATION TECHNIQUE

If you have not drawn up goals for your personal and professional life, try it. If you feel you don't *need* goals to succeed, try this: Think ahead ten years. Where will you be if you make no changes to your present career, lifestyle, education, investment portfolio, etc.? How old will you and your family be? What education will the children be able to afford? What job will you be working at? How much money will you be earning? What will you own? What hobbies will you have? What high points will you be able to look back on? If you're happy with what you see, you probably *don't* need goals. That's where you'll be. But don't kid yourself. If you're not saving money now, or not spending time with the family now, or not attending university now, what makes you think you *will* in the future? We all tend to procrastinate, and if we're not doing things now, it's unlikely we'll be doing those things in the future. Unless we set goals now and *start* now.

If you're not satisfied with what you see when looking ten years ahead, repeat the process. But this time assume that your "dreams" have come true. What does this new scenario look like ten years down the road? You may see a different person, with greater skills, accomplishments, interests and personal achievements. If you prefer this to the first scenario, draw up specific goals for yourself, and plan now how you're going to reach those goals. Almost anything can be accomplished in ten years. The hardest part is figuring out what you want and getting started.

CHARACTERISTICS OF GOALS

Briefly, here are some basics about goal-setting that you should keep in mind:

• *Put your goals in writing.* Otherwise, they're just dreams or wishes. If they're realistic, they can always be expressed in words. Writing them down makes you *focus* on them and provides commitment.

• *Make sure they're realistic.* Check them like this: Can they be reached by anyone with the same abilities and opportunities as you? If so, they're realistic. Avoid pie-in-the-sky goals which are beyond your reach. You might break them into sub-goals to see if they are realistic. For example, if saving $65,000 requires that you salt away $8,000 per month, is this within your control? Behind every goal is a plan as to how you expect to achieve it. If the plan is not workable, the goal is not achievable.

• *Be specific.* You have to be able to measure them so don't write down vague goals such as "to be happy," "to be fulfilled," "to be rich" or "to be intellectually mature." Think of the things that would make you happy or fulfilled and put them down in concrete terms. For example, a measurable goal would be "to attain the position of Principal in a suburban high school by May 31, 1996" or "to be qualified to assume the position of area superintendent by Sept. 1, 1997." Be sure your goals have a deadline.

• *List your goals in order of priority.* You may not be able to accomplish them all. Which ones are most important to you? Work on these first.

• *Make sure that your goals are compatible with each other* and that they are compatible with goals of your spouse or family members, too. One of your goals could involve starting your own private school while you are still employed full-time. Another goal could be to spend more quality time with your family. The two may not be compatible. Which one is more important to you? Can one of them be changed? Can one be temporarily sacrificed? Can you achieve both by selecting a less demanding business? Remember that it's personal goals that provide meaning and direction to your life.

MAKING YOUR GOALS ACHIEVABLE

One of the most frequent errors people make when setting goals is to make them too vague. You must be specific. Quantify them if possible, with a definite date to aim for. For example,

Don't say	Say
a lot of money	$64,000 saved by January 15,1995
lovely home	a $250,000, 4-bedroom split-level home in White Plains by Dec. 1, 1998
a promotion	Assistant Superintendent by Jan. 1, 1997
read a lot more	read one leadership book each month
attend seminars	attend one seminar each quarter (and specify topics)
vacation	a 3-week vacation in Maui in Oct., 1994
a new car	a 1998 Cadillac Seville,fully equipped, by Oct. 15, 1997

Goals are seldom achieved without conscious effort—and sometimes sacrifice—on your part. Are you willing to sacrifice short-term benefits for long-term rewards? Reflect on what it is you would really like to achieve. Be specific. Put it in a time frame, and adjust that time frame if the short-term goals become unrealistic. Then reduce your goals—and your plan—to written statements. Then adhere to that plan.

DEVELOP PROFESSIONAL GOALS

I have been using the term "personal" goals, and using examples such as saving money, taking courses, buying houses, etc. But the same process can be used for professional goals. For example, you might reflect on what major tasks you want to accomplish during the year. Record them in a planning binder or notebook. Make them specific, such as "To establish a study center for students from 5 p.m. to 6 p.m. three times per week in a neighborhood church basement by February 1, 1996," or "To establish a summer reading program for students in grades 6 through 8 by June 1, 1997."

Next, develop a strategy for achieving each of the goals. For example, if you are going to institute a study center by April 1, list point by point each step (sub-goals) in your plan. Record target dates for each step. For example, some of the steps might be:

- Prepare a proposal for the instalment of a study center in a local church to help students from "shaky" families study three afternoons per week, pointing out how grades and behavior are expected to improve with a minimal investment. Proposal to be ready for submission to the Superintendent by September 1, 1995.

- Meet with three pastors of local churches concerning the possibility of using a room for the new study center, outlining the requirements and the need for a respected volunteer to conduct the program. Meetings to be completed by November 1, 1995.

- Both the site and the person selected to operate the study center to be decided upon by December 1, 1995.

- Selection of volunteers to tutor at the study center (from among the local college, PTA, National Honor Society students) by January 1, 1996.

The steps may include the selection of someone at the school to coordinate the volunteer efforts, the provision of textbooks and materials, the encouragement of teachers to participate in the program, the announcement and publicity of the new center, notes of appreciation, etc.

Review your completed action plan, question whether the target dates are realistic, revise where necessary, and commit yourself to spending time each week working on the goal-related activities.

If you are using a "Taylor Time Planner," the days are broken into half-hour intervals for recording the actual time you will be working on the project, as illustrated in the next chapter. Don't attempt to fill in the actual times any more than two weeks in advance or you may have to do a lot of rescheduling. But you can record your weekly goals throughout the entire year — or at least for six months. This ensures that every week you will be spending *some* time on a priority task that will lead directly to one of your goals.

Those activities necessary to accomplish your goals, through the planning and scheduling process, must end up in your weekly planning calendar. You can *plan* long range, but you cannot *perform* long range. This scheduling process, which ensures that goals are achieved, will be covered in more detail in the next chapter.

Chapter 4

Scheduling: The Bridge Between Goals And Accomplishment

OUR NATURAL TENDENCIES

Managing time effectively is a difficult process, since it contravenes our natural tendencies.

We tend to spend more time on the things we enjoy doing at the expense of those tasks we find distasteful. Drawing up the master schedule or writing a major report for the Superintendent may be instrumental in initiating progressive programs, for example, but if we hate writing reports, we tend to do other things less productive and delay or skip the report writing.

We tend to work on the easy tasks before we start the difficult ones. It is only natural to take the path of least resistance. If a project is complex or will take a lot of time to complete, it is likely to be delayed. So if we need to develop a comprehensive new program as well as a one-day inservice presentation, guess which one gets tackled first? If the presentation can be polished off in a few hours, it gets the priority treatment, even though it may not be the priority. Rationalization also makes this tendency more palatable. "After all," we may reason, "if we get this easy task out of the way first, there's nothing to distract us from the important task." But of course there will *always* be distractions.

We tend to work on other peoples' priorities before we spend time on our own priorities. This is the "nice guy" attitude, which really reflects a lack of respect for our own time. For example, if someone asks to meet us at a time when we were planning to work on a task of our own, we frequently agree, delaying our own priorities rather than disappoint the other person.

For example, the Director of Pupil Personnel wants to meet with you, at an inconvenient time, to talk with you, prior to the interviewing process, about the characteristics of the person to replace a retired reading teacher. He's being "nudged" by the superintendent to get things moving. You're tied up for the next two days with parent meetings, classroom observations, etc. Do you say "Yes" to him and readjust your tight schedule or do you arrange to meet him at a time more convenient to you and the people you serve?

We tend to work on projects that bring an immediate reward—whether it is money or recognition—before those for which gratification is delayed. We are living in an "instant" generation, putting off things we want most for things we want at the moment. Although ineffective, it's a natural tendency. After all, we like to feel good so it's tempting to work on something that will provide that reward quickly.

We tend to work on the sure things before we tackle those things for which the outcome is less certain. In general, we are not risk-takers; we enjoy our comfort zones and like to tackle those tasks that we know will bring success—even though the potential of those other things may be much greater.

We tend to work on urgent items before those that are not urgent. All tasks that confront us can be classified as one of the following:

- Urgent and important.
- Urgent and unimportant.
- Not urgent and important.
- Not urgent and unimportant

Most priorities are not urgent when they first appear, while many unimportant tasks are urgent at the outset. Consequently, we work on unimportant things simply because they're urgent, while important items are held in abeyance — until *they* become urgent as well. So we're caught up in the tyranny of the urgent, under stress, racing the clock and fighting to keep our heads above water.

A general guideline for handling the different tasks is as follows:

*   If it's urgent and important, do it now.
*   If it's urgent and unimportant, either delegate it or let it slide.
*   If it's not urgent and important, plan when best to do it and schedule it into your planner.
*   If it's not urgent and unimportant, leave it.

Finally, *we tend to work on those things that are scheduled in our planners before we start the things on our "to do" lists.* Lists of things to do are intentions; but scheduled blocks of time in our planning calendars are commitments. Rarely do we forget or delay appointments or meetings that are scheduled for specific times. But things included on a to-do list are often overlooked. Frequently, those missed activities are far more important than the scheduled appointments.

This last tendency to work on scheduled activities can help you be more productive *if* you schedule priority activities, not simply people. Don't leave priority, goal-related activities on a "things-to-do" list. Break the complex tasks into manageable chunks and schedule time for them in your planner. Tackle the unpleasant tasks during your prime time, when you feel more energetic and mentally alert. For most people this is early in the morning.

It takes self-discipline to say "no" to urgent but unimportant activities. And it takes self-discipline to work for an hour or two on unpleasant tasks that will take hundreds of hours to complete. But it's a lot easier when you schedule them into your planner as appointments with yourself.

SELECTING A PLANNER

A planner, diary, calendar or whatever you wish to call it, should do more than simply tell you what day it is. Basically, a planner should

- display your annual goals so you never lose sight of where you're heading;

- supply enough space to actually schedule time to work on those goal-related activities;

- remind you of appointments, assignments due, meetings and special events such as birthdays;

- list the multitude of things that you have to do that day or that week so you won't forget them;

- provide space for scheduling evening and weekend activities so your work won't crowd out personal commitments.

There are other things that planners could do for you. But don't choose a planner with all the bells and whistles if you never use bells and whistles. The planner should fit your personal management style, not the reverse. Some of the more analytical people prefer a day-at-a-glance, perhaps because they like detailed records of everything. Others prefer a month-at-a-glance because they're more interested in the overall picture and long-term results and don't want to get locked into the daily nitty gritty. I prefer the week-at-a-glance, so I can concentrate on detail, yet have an idea of how the week is shaping up.

It provides space to schedule activities without the constant flipping of pages necessary in the day-at-a-glance planners. A. Roger Merrill, in his book *Connections: Quadrant II Time Management*, suggests that "the week is a complete little patch out of the fabric of life. It has the weekend; it has the evening; it has the workday." It's difficult to balance your life on a daily basis, but a weekly schedule puts things in perspective.

You should give careful thought to the selection of a planner, since it's within its pages that you organize your life. Select one you feel comfortable with. And don't be afraid to try different types and change part way through the year—until you find one that is compatible with your lifestyle.

I recommend you use a larger planner than the pocket size and schedule all activities and events; record all birthdays and anniversaries; describe all trips and vacations; include rough maps of how to get to places; list items to take to staff meetings and conferences, etc. Then your planning calendar will also serve as a record of where you have been and what you have done, complete with reusable information for the future.

Select one that has enough space for the entries yet is portable enough to toss into your briefcase or purse. It should have time segments from 7:00 a.m. to 9:00 p.m. or later (for recording personal commitments). It should contain the total year so you can plan well ahead. Also, have space for those daily "things to do" that don't merit assignment to any particular time slot. Choose one that will work for *you*.

More important than the planner you select is the way you use it. Keep your goals highlighted there, as well as your "to do" list, important telephone numbers, assignments due, commitments made, important events to remember *and* scheduled blocks of time for yourself. Don't be afraid to record information in your planner, including evening and weekend plans. People who simply use it as a calendar—to tell whether a holiday falls on a Monday or a Tuesday—are making a mistake. The more you use it the more valuable it becomes and the more organized you will be.

USING YOUR PLANNER EFFECTIVELY

If you start work with a list of 10 items to do and stop at night with a list of 15, including the original 10, you may be a victim of the "To Do" list fallacy. A list of things to do provides no commitment to get things done.

Instead, separate the priority, high payback activities from the items of lesser importance and schedule these "must do" items directly into your planning calendar along with your meetings. For instance, the development of a policy manual should never remain on a "To Do" list. Block out the time needed in your planner, let's say between 2:30 p.m. and 4:00 p.m., and treat it as though it were a meeting with the Superintendent. Close your door and have calls intercepted if that's what you would do if it *were* a meeting with someone else. But allow a little extra time for those unavoidable interruptions that are bound to occur. If you schedule several of these meetings with yourself during the week, you will accomplish those priority jobs and increase your effectiveness.

"To Do" lists are fine for grocery shopping; but if you're a results-oriented person, a scheduled commitment is a must. Don't be discouraged if some of your scheduled activities have to be changed. A schedule is a guideline and must be flexible. But resist changing your schedule simply to accommodate tasks of no greater importance than your originally planned activity. If a book salesperson shows up unexpectedly, for instance, don't abandon your priorities in favor of an impromptu meeting. Block periods of time in your planning calendar with the intent of following through with them. But don't stop scheduling even if your plans have to be frequently altered. Doctors don't stop scheduling office appointments simply because they are frequently called out on emergencies.

GIVE PRIORITY TO PRIORITIES

The first thing you schedule in your planner should be blocks of time to work on your goal-related activities. This will ensure that you are working on the 20% of the activities that will produce 80% of your results.

The "Taylor Time Planner," available from Harold Taylor Time Consultants Inc., was designed to enable its user to continue to focus on those original priority goals throughout the year. There is a single page near the front of the planner for the current year's goals. (*See* Exhibit 1.) List here those priority projects which you want to accomplish during the year. Not

1993 GOALS

In the spaces below, list the major accomplishments you wish to achieve during the year, along with the target dates.

Each week, enter into the "This Week's Priority" section of your planner the goal(s) you plan to work towards that week.

Then, in specific, daily time slots, schedule time to work on those goal-related activities.

As you reach each annual goal, check it off in the left hand margin.

✔	ANNUAL GOALS	Target Date

EXHIBIT 1
Annual Goals Form

the routine jobs. Not those obligations that do little to further your school's priorities. Only those key goals.

They could be the ones you have been putting off year after year because you simply haven't had the time. These goals could be personal as well as professional. They could include the writing of a book, the redecorating of a home, or a trip to Europe.

In order to determine the target date (recorded in the column to the right of the goal), estimate how many hours it would take to complete the task. In some cases, this is impossible to determine accurately. If so, simply guess, then add up to 50% to be on the safe side. For example, if you feel it could take 100 hours of solid writing to finish a book, make it 150 hours. Then divide this figure by the number of weeks you plan to work that year. For example, if you work 50 weeks, then the number of hours each week that you will have to work on your goal-related activity should be three. Since it is difficult to work steadily for three hours on any activity, break this into two sessions of 1½ hours each. To accomplish your goal of writing a book, you would have to spend 1½ hours twice per week in order to complete it by the end of the year. If this amount of time is unrealistic, set the goal for the end of the following year and work half as long each week. Don't be impatient; be realistic.

Let's assume you have set a goal, recorded the target date, and have estimated that you would have to spend two blocks of time (of 1½ hours) each week throughout the year. Turning to the planner pages, you will find a section to the left headed "This Week's Priority" (Exhibit 2). Here you record the goal you plan to work toward that week. For instance, "write book" or "paint house" or "institute study center." Your priority, goal-oriented "To Do" list is always kept separately from those routine and urgent items that pop out of the woodwork daily. You will note there is a "Things To Do" column below the "Priority" section on the planning pages for your regular, changing list of "Things To Do."

The continual recording of your major goals on each weekly page keeps your original intentions in mind. Each week you must now schedule an actual time in your weekly planner to work on that particular task. Treat these blocks of time as though they were appointments with important people (in fact they *are*, appointments with *yourself*). By now you will already have appointments, meetings, etc., scheduled in your planner. You will have to work around these. But once your priority, goal-related activities have been scheduled, resist any temptation to use this time for less important "spur of the moment" things. Pretend they are appointments with your surgeon. Few people would delay lifesaving surgery.

This method of actually determining the amount of time it will take to accomplish a goal forces you to be realistic. If you had ten goals, for instance, all requiring two hours each week to accomplish, it is unlikely you would be able to steal 20 hours each week to work on those special projects. You would have no time for your regular jobs (or for family time if you planned to work on them in the evening). But there's always next year. Boil those goals down to the few really meaningful accomplishments which would give you the greatest return on invested time. A scheduled week may resemble Exhibit 3. Be realistic. Leave spaces to accommodate the unexpected and to allow time for those items on the "to do" section.

If you don't want to use a "Taylor Time Planner," don't let that stop you. Use a separate piece of paper for your goals, glue it into your planner, and schedule blocks of time each week to work on those goals. (You must have a planner that breaks each day into time segments, however. Little blank squares for the days will not work.) Your planner is your most important time management tool, so choose it carefully. Get into the habit of referring to it every morning. Follow it like a road map. Look at it again in the evening and make any necessary changes to the next day's plan.

Eliminate New Year's resolutions and replace them with a few meaningful goals. Get them into writing and transpose them into your time planner. Then schedule time each week to work on activities that will lead you to those goals. Concentrate your efforts on those few relevant tasks each week.

A magnifying glass will focus the sun's energy onto one spot, burning holes in objects and causing combustible materials to burst into flame. Similarly, goals will focus your energy onto a few major activities, magnifying the value of your results.

THIS WEEK'S PRIORITY

JANUARY	FEBRUARY	MARCH	APRIL	MAY
S M T W T F S	S M T W T F S	S M T W T F S	S M T W T F S	S M T W T F S
1 2 3 4	1	1 2 3 4 5 6 7	1 2 3 4	1 2
5 6 7 8 9 10 11	2 3 4 5 6 7 8	8 9 10 11 12 13 14	5 6 7 8 9 10 11	3 4 5 6 7 8 9
12 13 14 15 16 17 18	9 10 11 12 13 14 15	15 16 17 18 19 20 21	12 13 14 15 16 17 18	10 11 12 13 14 15 16
19 20 21 22 23 24 25	16 17 18 19 20 21 22	22 23 24 25 26 27 28	19 20 21 22 23 24 25	17 18 19 20 21 22 23
26 27 28 29 30 31	23 24 25 26 27 28 29	29 30 31	26 27 28 29 30	24 25 26 27 28 29 30
				31

MONDAY MARCH	TUESDAY MARCH	WEDNESDAY MARCH
Follow ups:	Follow ups:	Follow ups:
69	70	71

THINGS TO DO:

Monday	Tuesday	Wednesday
7	7	7
-30-	-30-	-30-
8	8	8
-30-	-30-	-30-
9	9	9
-30-	-30-	-30-
10	10	10
-30-	-30-	-30-
11	11	11
-30-	-30-	-30
12	12	12
-30-	-30-	-30-
1	1	1
-30-	-30-	-30-
2	2	2
-30-	-30-	-30-
3	3	3
-30-	-30-	-30-
4	4	4
-30-	-30-	-30-
5	5	5
-30-	-30-	-30-
6	6	6
-30-	-30-	-30-
7	7	7
-30-	-30-	-30-
8	8	8
-30-	-30-	-30-
9	9	9

PERSONAL:

....
....
....
....
....
....
....
....
....
....
....
....
....
....

(continued)

EXHIBIT 2

JUNE S M T W T F S	**JULY** S M T W T F S	**AUGUST** S M T W T F S	**SEPTEMBER** S M T W T F S	**OCTOBER** S M T W T F S	**NOVEMBER** S M T W T F S	**DECEMBER** S M T W T F S

THURSDAY MARCH	FRIDAY MARCH	SATURDAY MARCH	SUNDAY MARCH
Follow ups:	Follow ups:	Follow ups:	Follow ups:
86	87	88	89
	7	7	7
	-30-	-30-	-30-
	8	8	8
	-30-	-30-	-30-
	9	9	9
	-30-	-30-	-30-
	10	10	10
	-30-	-30-	-30-
	11	11	11
	-30-	-30-	-30-
	12	12	12
	-30-	-30-	-30-
	1	1	1
	-30-	-30-	-30-
	2	2	2
	-30	-30-	-30-
	3	3	3
	-30-	-30-	-30-
	4	4	4
	-30-	-30-	-30-
	5	5	5
	-30-	-30-	-30-
	6	6	6
	-30-	-30-	-30-
	7	7	7
	-30-	-30-	-30-
	8	8	8
	-30-	-30-	-30-
	9	9	9

EXHIBIT 2
"Week-At-A-Glance" Planner

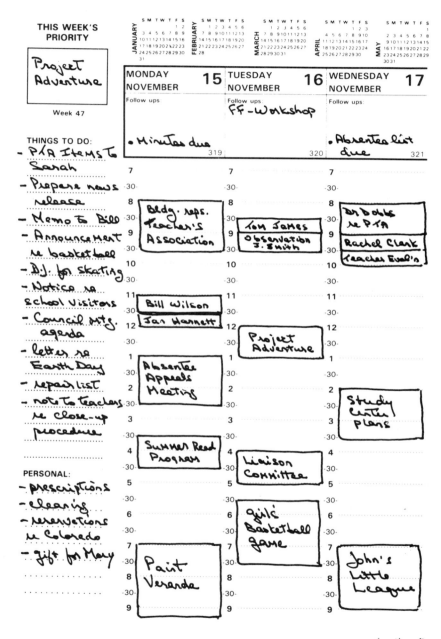

(continued)

EXHIBIT 3

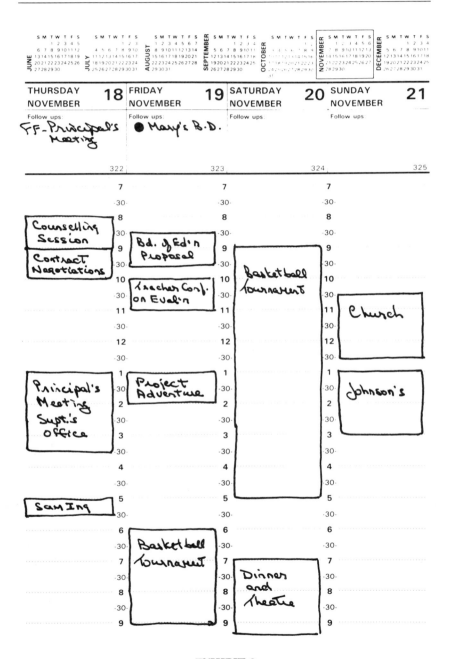

EXHIBIT 3
Planner With Activities Scheduled

Chapter 5

Controlling
Interruptions

THE VALUE OF A QUIET HOUR

There are really only three steps to accomplishment: Set goals, schedule time to work on those goals, and then follow through on your plan. The problem is in the actual follow-through or "doing" stage. Interfering with the actual work are a myriad of interruptions, crises, rush jobs, meetings, and the routine but essential activities that consume your time.

Scheduling more time than you think the task will take allows for interruptions. And leaving plenty of unscheduled time in your planner facilitates working on those unanticipated priorities that materialize each day. But you will still have to curb interruptions as much as possible in order to be effective.

To do this you should schedule quiet hours coinciding with those times you are working on priority, goal-related tasks. I hesitate to use the term "quiet hour" since no hour is entirely "quiet" at school *or* at home. But it's the accepted term, and refers to the attempt to maintain that block of time that you have set aside for a specific task *relatively* free of interruptions. You won't eliminate *all* interruptions, and for that reason I recommend you schedule up to 50% more time than you think you will need to complete a job. But you will be able to eliminate *most* interruptions once you make up your mind that you deserve as much respect as anyone else. I say this because many people feel uncomfortable having calls and visitors intercepted when there's no one in their office with them.

There's nothing wrong with closing your door and having a "meeting with yourself" so you can spend some undisturbed time on priority tasks. But some people feel guilty. They think they're deceiving others by suggesting they are with someone, when in actual fact they are alone. And no wonder. Some people go to great lengths to convince other people that they are involved in something else. I've heard of one person who tells his secretary he's going out on consultation, when "Consultation" is the name of a boat he owns. Another leaves word that he's on course, when it's actually a golf course. When you get to the point of having to deceive others into thinking you're doing something other than spending quiet time alone, the quiet time will not be effective. Too much time will be spent on the deception and the concomitant feeling of guilt, and not enough on the task at hand.

It's a fact of life. People are more productive when they can work at something undisturbed. At least one hour each day spent in relative seclusion, away from ringing telephones and drop-in visitors, will increase your effectiveness. So make it part of your daily routine. Don't overdo it. If your door is *always* closed people will ignore it and walk in anyway. And make sure people know how long you will be tied up. A word to your secretary, or a sign on the door, "Available at 3 p.m.," is sufficient. Also, be sensitive to the schedules of others. Classroom teachers, whose time is structured, may need access to you during *their* breaks. Don't let your quiet hours coincide with the only times other people are to see you.

Above all, don't feel guilty that you're making yourself unavailable to students, staff, outsiders, for a period of time. If you're interrupted in what you're doing for only one minute, it will take another three minutes to recover. A "quiet hour," where no interruptions are allowed except emergencies, will magnify your effectiveness. Fight for it. If people ignore your closed door, post a sign on it. If your superiors object, show them the *results* of that quiet hour. There *will* be results. Those people who have gotten up early and worked for an hour at the kitchen table will realize this. You can get about three times as much accomplished when interruptions are eliminated. This assumes you don't interrupt *yourself*. The temptation to do this is great. We're used to being interrupted so much we miss it when it doesn't happen. Discipline yourself. Just once, make up your mind to work at a project for a whole hour without stopping to take a walk, a stretch, a coffee or to daydream or stare out the window. The results of that hour will be your reward, and your incentive to do it again the next day.

Many administrators feel it is impossible to have a quiet hour and still be caring, compassionate individuals. That the door should be open at all times. That they should be fully accessible to everyone at all times. But think for a moment. Have you ever closed the door and had your calls intercepted when you had a meeting with the Superintendent, a teacher, a parent, or a student? Have you ever been unavailable because you were home sick, or at a conference, or attending a school function, or making the rounds? Were you considered uncaring as a result?

The fact is, it is impossible to be available to all people at all times. Is it too much to ask that you devote an hour or so each day to *yourself*, working on projects that would benefit those same students, teachers, and parents?

Don't lose sight of the *reason* for a "quiet hour;" it's to allow you to work on those important projects. Don't waste this valuable time on trivial tasks. If you schedule correctly, you will not have more than one or two hours of "quiet time" in any one day. Make sure there are plenty of blank spaces in your time planner each day. After all, you need plenty of time to deal with those "interruptions" that you have defended against. The point is not to ignore them. Interruptions are part of our job. What we are attempting to do is protect blocks of time—meetings with ourselves—during which time we are relatively inaccessible to the demands of other people. But we must still meet those demands later. If they are *emergencies*, they may even preempt our quiet time. But if they do, there are those "spaces" in our planning calendar where our *tasks* can be rescheduled.

In order to get a quiet hour, some people arrive at the office one hour before starting time—an ideal time, since there's no obligation to answer the telephone or leave your door open. It's tempting to pick up the telephone, however; so to make this work you must have the willpower to ignore ringing telephones. There's also the danger of extending your working hours. Work expands to fill the time available for it (Parkinson's Law), so working longer hours will not necessarily make you more effective. Other administrators find it helpful to spend some time in a more secluded part of the building where they are less likely to be distracted.

In defense of the "quiet hour," let me relate a story, that was told to me, of a director of a parachurch organization who was accused of ignoring the needs of his people while giving preferential treatment to paperwork. "You call these letters and reports inanimate objects?," he exclaimed. "We have over 100 missionaries abroad whose only access to me, to you, and to our facilities is through these letters and reports. On the other hand, you have access to me day and night, in person or by phone. These are not inanimate objects," he admonished them. "These are *people*."

The important paperwork you deal with daily is also a "person." It deserves the same respect as a person sitting in your office, so never feel guilty about having calls and visitors intercepted while you give it your attention.

DEALING WITH DROP-INS

It's one thing to convince yourself that quiet hours makes sense, and that you should have them coincide with those blocks of time in which you have scheduled your priority tasks. But how do you physically keep those calls and drop-ins from interrupting you? After all, most administrators do work amid scores of people, telephones, and equipment. Some don't even have offices. And what about the superintendent? Does a closed door keep him or her out?

If you have followed the foregoing advice, you at least have been able to *have* a quiet hour. Now let's see just how "quiet" we can make it. Your environment does have an effect on quiet, so if you are working in an open-office concept, make it as private as possible by adding dividers and potted plants. Get out of the line of sight of people passing your desk. If your eyes meet, it's human instinct to give a word of greeting, which in turn leads to an exchange of niceties, which, in turn, frequently leads to a full-fledged conversation.

You cannot afford to get sidetracked during your quiet hour, so avoid the initial eye contact. The people who really want to see and talk to you will peek around the partition or divider so don't be concerned about feeling antisocial. And remember, you are free to walk out from behind that divider whenever you want—hopefully not during your quiet hour. I realize it's difficult to keep your mind on your work when you are working in an open-office environment with telephones ringing, people chatting, and computer printers clattering. But you can do it, if you make up your mind that you are going to concentrate on what you are doing. Your ability to concentrate is increased with positive effort and reduced by allowing yourself to be diverted. It can be represented by the following formula:

$$\text{Ability to Concentrate} = \frac{\text{Positive Effort}}{\text{Diversion}}$$

Keep the positive effort high by consciously focusing your thoughts on the job at hand. It is amazing how much of the environment you can shut out of your mind when you are highly motivated to get on with the job. Have an organized work area with all the information and tools necessary to get the job done. And be aware that your susceptibility to diversion increases the longer you're at the job. Don't schedule too long a period without a break. Get away from your desk periodically and clear the cobwebs. Schedule the most difficult tasks when you're at your peak, perhaps first thing in the morning.

You can be productive in spite of a lack of privacy once you set your mind to it.

A closed door will not keep out legitimate interruptions. In fact, it sometimes only succeeds in slowing down the more timid intruders. If someone does barge in, ask what it is they want. If it's a crisis that demands your immediate attention, go to it. Hopefully, it will not consume the entire block of quiet time. If it does, you'll have to reschedule. But don't allow lengthy interruptions unless the situation is more important than the task it is displacing. Signing forms, reviewing or proofreading reports can usually wait. In fact, many so-called "crises" could also wait an hour or so without dire consequences.

Encourage people to make appointments to see you. If you persist in allowing everyone in the community to walk in on you at their own convenience, you are not only signaling that you don't value your time but you will not be able to serve them as effectively.

WATCH THOSE SELF-INTERRUPTIONS

Isn't it odd that none of us interrupt others needlessly, yet we all experience superfluous interruptions ourselves? None of us make unnecessary calls, talk too long, engage in idle chitchat, cause disturbances by talking too loudly, barge unannounced into offices, make trivial requests, set unrealistic deadlines, circulate trivial paperwork, drag out meetings, yet we are constantly having these time wasters imposed upon us.

The truth is, it is easier to find fault with others than with ourselves. We are all guilty to varying degrees, and in order to increase efficiency within our organizations we must look at ourselves objectively. We must be aware of what we are doing and manage ourselves by ridding ourselves of poor work habits which disrupt others.

We cannot change our behavior unless we admit that it needs changing. So study yourself for one day, looking for time wasters such as those mentioned previously. Are you calling the same person four or five times a day, shouting across the office instead of using the intercom, making several trips to the copier or supply cabinet and interrupting others in the process? If you can find nothing wrong with your behavior, ask those who work with you.

Time management is self-management. If everyone would become aware of how he or she interrupts others, and changed his or her behavior accordingly, efficiency would soar.

If you find you are guilty, here are a few ways to reduce those interruptions:

- Accumulate your questions or assignments if they're not urgent and interrupt the people only once or twice during the day.

- When you think of someone you have to call, jot down the name, number and item, but resist making the call immediately. Other items that need discussing may come to mind later.

- Resist the urge to act impulsively. Keep a "copy" folder in which to toss papers, reducing trips to the copier.

- Keep a folder for those people you normally visit frequently (or who visit you) and accumulate those items requiring their attention.

- Communicate with your secretary. Meet with him/her daily, preferably in the morning. Don't walk out of the office without saying when you'll be back; don't close your door without saying how long you'll be tied up.

- Don't set unrealistic deadlines. Don't ask for everything today if you don't need it for a week. But be sure you do place a deadline on all assignments.

- Keep ample supplies, stationery, etc., at your work station to avoid frequent trips.

- Respect other peoples' "quiet hours" and closed doors. If they come in early to get work done, cooperate by not socializing during their prime time.

- Be explicit when making assignments so there's no confusion as to what you want done and when it's to be completed. If directions are not clear, you're begging for interruptions.

• Don't use your own need for a break as an excuse to interrupt others; they may be in an opposite frame of mind.

KEEP A "DELEGATION RECORD"

One of the advantages of the **Delegation Record** (*see* Exhibit 4) is that it eliminates incessant interruptions to yourself and others. When working on a letter, report or other project, thoughts unrelated to the task continually pop into our minds. The tendency is to grab for the phone or call to someone across the room or immediately switch to another task. Constant diversions such as these make our workday inefficient. By jotting the thought into the appropriate section of the **Delegation Record** for later action, we don't forget it and don't get sidetracked.

Most of the things we think of involve other people. If it's an assignment that will involve considerable time on the part of someone else, jot it in the main "Delegation" section. If it's a small task that you want done or something to communicate to that person, use the "Instant Task" section. It could be a question you have to ask, a reminder, information to give, or a follow-up of some kind. Getting it onto the form frees your mind to continue concentrating on the task at hand with no fear of forgetting.

Later in the day, when the current task is completed, you can follow up on those items you thought of during the day. You can interrupt staff members only once, and review several items at the same time. Be sure to get a commitment as to the date the assignment will be completed. Jot a reminder in the "Follow-up" section of your time planner on that date so you'll remember to follow up. Check off those items in the "Instant Task" section once you have reviewed them.

Keep a separate **Delegation Record** for everyone who reports to you or works with you on a regular basis. It will become a permanent record of the assignments given, adherence to deadlines, and performance. Make a note in the "Comments"

DELEGATION RECORD

MANAGER_____MONTH_____

Date Assigned	Assignment	Due Date	Date Completed	Comments

"INSTANT" TASKS   check box at right when completed

©1988 Harold Taylor Time Consultants Inc.

EXHIBIT 4
Delegation Record

section as to how effectively the task was completed. The form can be a handy reference at evaluation time.

The **Delegation Record** will ensure that you are distributing the assignments evenly among your staff members. A long list of assignments on Joe's form and only a few for John indicate that you may be inadvertently piling most of the jobs onto one person.

SUMMARY

Have as much respect for your own time as you have for other peoples' time. Without quiet hours it could take twice as long to complete a project, make it impossible to concentrate on the task at hand, reduce the quality of workmanship, and increase stress. Here is a summary of points to keep in mind when scheduling periodic quiet hours:

- Don't overdo it. One or two times during the day for periods not exceeding 1½ hours each should be sufficient. If you close your door too often for too long a period of time, people will either ignore it and walk in anyway, or they will be less efficient themselves because of your unavailability.

- Let your secretary or assistant know when you will be free again. Leave complete instructions as to how to intercept calls. (For example, have the secretary field calls from parents and others, obtain enough information, and either handle it personally, refer the call to someone closer to the issue, or make an appointment for a callback.) At home ask your spouse or children to do the same.

- Don't waste the quiet hour by working on trivial tasks. Work only on priority jobs that you have scheduled in advance.

- Make sure you have all the materials you will need *before* you close the door. Don't keep popping out of your office or the advantage of a quiet hour is lost.

- Pick a time that works best for you. It could be at a time when calls and visitors are usually at a low ebb. Or it could be first thing in the morning when you're at your mental peak. Or, if there is no best time, vary the time each day.

- Schedule these quiet hours at least a week ahead so your calendar doesn't get filled with "people" appointments, leaving no time for yourself.

- Make it as quiet as possible. If you can't turn off the telephone, consider using a library, boardroom, empty classroom or some remote spot that doesn't have a telephone.

- Return all calls promptly after your quiet hour is over. If you don't, people will stop respecting your quiet hour.

- If you have not finished the assignment by the time the quiet hour is over, schedule another future appointment with yourself. If you have a deadline to work toward, you will work more efficiently. Dragging out the quiet hour defeats its purpose. (Exception: If another five minutes or so will finish the job.)

- Don't feel guilty. You are not ignoring the needs of people; you are working on priority projects that involve people.

- Respect other peoples' quiet hours as well.

But how can we have a quiet hour when we don't have an office? Here are a few suggestions:

- Get away from your desk. Use a spare office or vacant classroom for an hour. Other "quiet" areas include the library, the cafeteria (but not at lunch time) or even your car in the parking lot.

- If you can't leave the office area once you're there, can you work at home for the first hour of every day? If not, can a staggered hour (or flexible hour) system help out?

Arriving early, before many staff members arrive and before the outside calls start coming in, can decrease the interruptions.

• Can you reduce interruptions for an hour by taking a late (or early) lunch and working at your desk during the "normal" lunch hour when most people are away?

• If the above strategies are impossible, can you use the buddy system? Ask another person to take all your calls for an hour and you can take all his or her calls for an hour in return.

• If all else fails, make your "open area" as private as possible by adding screens or plants. Face away from the main traffic flow while you are working. Avoid eye contact with passersby. And use your power of concentration.

Chapter 6

Managing The Telephone

MANAGING STARTS WITH PLANNING

Time management consultant Stephen Young claims the average time consumed by an unplanned telephone call is 12 minutes, while the time consumed by a planned call is only seven minutes. A saving of five minutes is therefore possible every time an agenda is drawn up before dialing a number.

The **Telephone and Visitor's Log** (Exhibit 5) or a simple steno pad would facilitate note-taking during calls. The agenda could be a simple list of the two or three points you want to make during the conversation. Introducing the conversation with a courteous, but businesslike, "Hi, Bill. Jim Elliott here. Sorry to interrupt you. I have three quick questions to ask . . ." might get the "telephone meeting" quickly on track. If you make a dozen calls each day and save five minutes on each call, you have just redeemed a full hour to use on something else.

Planning does not mean grabbing for the telephone every time you think of someone you want to talk to. Planning involves jotting that thought down on your telephone log so you won't forget, and continuing with the job at hand. By the time you make the call you may have thought of several other things you want to speak to the same person about. Accumulating your ideas or questions and making one call instead of two or three is a real time saver—for you *and* the other person.

Your telephone could eliminate some time-consuming appointments. When someone asks for an appointment to see you, find out what he or she wants. Chances are you'll be able to settle it right there on the phone.

This could apply to parents with problems. Find out the details on the phone. Don't go running out to put out fires until you know all the facts. It could be that the parent, with a little guidance from you, could solve his or her own problem. Keep in mind that the parent's objective is not necessarily to see you in person, but to get some action or reassurance.

The phone can also be used to reduce the number of letters and memos. Many letters you receive are simply asking a question or requesting some information. Resist the urge to write back. Pick up the phone and give your answer verbally. It's usually faster, less expensive, and impresses the sender with your prompt reply. If you need written confirmation, fine. But don't write if you don't have to.

With written notes on a telephone log you have the material necessary if you have to refer back to your discussion. And with the separate "Action" section, you won't forget to follow up on any requests made during the conversation.

The telephone can be used for conference calls to avoid unnecessary and costly meetings. It can be used to confirm or remind people of appointments so you don't waste time. It can even reply for you through electronic messaging systems such as voice mailbox. Many people simply want to tell you something and don't need a personal response immediately. Why carry on a conversation at all if only one-way communication is required?

If the budget allows, investigate the various equipment options available: A speaker telephone to free your hands for work; flashing lights to avoid the nerve-jangling and disrupting bell; automatic dialing to save time looking up numbers. In addition, many people don't know how to use the phone system they do have. They are unaware of many of their system's features, such as silence buttons, redial, call forward-

TELEPHONE & VISITORS LOG

NAME _____

COMPANY _____

NUMBER _____

DATE _____

TIME _____

NATURE OF BUSINESS

CALL ☐

VISIT ☐

INITIATED BY:

MYSELF ☐

OTHER PARTY ☐

TIME: _____

LENGTH
OF
CALL
MINUTES

2 4 6 8 10 12 14 16 18 20 22 24

ACTION REQUIRED

© 1988 Harold Taylor Time Consultants Inc.

EXHIBIT 5

Telephone & Visitors Log

ing, intercom workings, voice messaging. If you have many people who have not been trained in the proper use of the telephone system, now might be a good time to organize a familiarization session.

Remember that the telephone is there to serve you, not the reverse. Control it. Don't be a slave to it. You'll be more effective as a result.

MAKE NOTES WHILE LISTENING

Use a "Telephone & Visitors Log" to record the caller's name and number, the date of the call, a brief summary of the reason for the call, and any action required as a result of it. Fill it out as you talk—it takes no longer than not making notes—and you'll never forget any necessary follow-ups. The action required section is at the right of the form, where it stands out. When you've completed the action, put an "X" through the notation. You could also note the date that action was taken for future reference.

This form prevents you from having to rely on your memory, ensures you get the caller's number in case you have to call back, and provides a permanent record of any promises, prices quoted, or other information which could be of use at a later date. (*See* Exhibit 5.)

The "Telephone & Visitors Log," which highlight's action required and summarizes relevant information, has the following advantages:

- *Reduces Interruption*. People have a tendency to interrupt you while you're listening on the telephone; but start writing while you are on the phone and people think you're busy and don't try to talk to you.

- *Increases Concentration*. While listening, you are exposed to distractions, including other people speaking loudly on *their* telephones. But it's virtually impossible to listen to a caller, make notes on the conversation, and even be aware of other people's voices.

* *Improves Memory.* Writing things down is an accepted technique of transferring information into long-term memory. You will be able to recall more information after having written it down.

* *Ensures Follow-up Action.* When you write down any action required on your part, it is impossible to have it "slip your mind." It stands out on the right-hand side of that form. Until it's crossed off, you know it's not done, so you can't forget to take action.

* *Provides a Written Record.* Many phone calls never result in written confirmation of items discussed, leaving yourself open to communication distortion afterwards. A written record protects your back in case the conversation is denied or distorted afterwards.

* *Eliminates Scraps of Paper.* People frequently scribble notes on scraps of paper which easily become lost or cause clutter. A form in a binder provides a tidy record of calls in chronological order.

* *Provides a Time Log.* The "Telephone & Visitors Log" has a facility for quickly recording the duration of the call (by circling the appropriate elapsed time). This facilitates keeping control of time spent on the telephone. Also, it pinpoints the long-winded callers!

* *Highlights Your Telephone Activity.* Systematic recording of calls provides hardcopy proof of the frequency and length of your calls. This could be used to justify voice messaging equipment, the screening of calls, staff assistance, etc. Also the need for a "quiet hour!"

* *Decreases Length of Call.* The form allows you to jot down the items you want to discuss before making the call. This planned agenda allows you to control the call without forgetting any items and frequently eliminates the necessity of another call.

* *Avoids Embarrassment.* When a stranger calls, it is easy to forget the person's name by the end of the conversa-

tion. Since this is the first thing you write on the form, you can refer to it during the call and when closing the conversation.

* *Serves as Reminder*. The headings at the top of the form prevent you from forgetting to ask the caller's number in case you have to call him/her back. Also, the caller's company name, date and time of call.

There could be other advantages to recording notes if such events as litigation or arbitration take place at a later date. The little effort required to make notes is more than offset by the inherent advantages. Although a scratch pad or notepad will suffice, a more formal form in a binder increases consistency of use and format and makes subsequent filing easier.

The "Perpetual" telephone log (*see* Exhibit 6) is used when calls to one person are frequent, as in the case of ongoing conversations with a parent. The advantage of this form is that the name, address, and telephone number of the person need only be recorded once, and all the calls and action taken can be viewed at a glance. These forms can be filed behind alphabetical tabs for easy reference. This form also facilitates recording of the total time spent talking with the same person.

USE THE TELEPHONE EFFICIENTLY

Keep conversations brief. Leave any socializing until after you've completed the business portion of the call. In fact, you'll find neither party has much time for small talk afterwards. It's simply used as a warmup before getting to the point of the call. To get down to business quickly, don't start by asking the caller how he is. He may take 10 minutes to tell you—after which it's your turn. Simply ask pleasantly "Hi, Jack, what can I do for you?" Chances are, he'll tell you. If you're good friends and you both have time to spare, you can exchange niceties afterwards. Treat a telephone conversation like you would a meeting, and appoint yourself chairperson. Keep it on track, and when the objective is reached, end the call. Always assume

PERPETUAL
TELEPHONE & VISITOR'S LOG

COMPANY _____   CONTACT _____

ADDRESS _____   INFO.

_____

TELEPHONE _____

DATE	TIME	ITEMS DISCUSSED	ELAPSED TIME	ACTION REQUIRED
			TIME: _____ LENGTH OF CALL MINUTES	
			TIME: _____ LENGTH OF CALL MINUTES	
			TIME: _____ LENGTH OF CALL MINUTES	
			TIME: _____ LENGTH OF CALL MINUTES	

EXHIBIT 6
Perpetual Telephone & Visitors Log

the other person is busy and end with something like "Well, I won't keep you, Bill. I know you're busy." It's unlikely he'll admit that he *isn't*. End the conversation politely, but promptly.

A minute or two in planning your calls could save three or four in execution. Don't phone on impulse. If the call can wait, jot down a reminder and continue with your work. Chances are you will think of something else you have to call that person about. Do this throughout the morning and make all your calls in a group, say between 11 a.m. and noon. Repeat the procedure in the afternoon.

HAVING CALLS INTERCEPTED

When having calls intercepted during your "quiet hours," it's important to do so without antagonizing the callers. *Don't* have your secretary ask who's calling. If you're busy, you're busy regardless of who's calling!

If someone asks "Could I speak to John Brown, please?," and the immediate response is "Could I ask who's calling?," the caller could easily get the impression that he or she is being screened to see if their name is important enough to warrant your time. If they are later told that you are tied up, they could be annoyed.

If you're going to have your calls intercepted at any time, do it this way. When the person asks if John Brown is there, have the secretary feed back the truth immediately. "Yes, he is" or "No, he isn't" or "Yes, but he's tied up right now," followed immediately by the question "Can I help you?" Then the caller knows that his or her name has nothing to do with the fact that you are tied up.

Incidentally, when *you* make a call, never force the other person's secretary to wheedle your name from you. *Announce* who's calling right at the outset. "Hello, this is Bill Smith, Principal of Wurthering Heights. Could I speak to John Brown, please?" This way, you will never be insulted.

When it's obvious that you must return the call personally, the secretary should find out the best time to reach the caller. A simple "When is the best time to call you back?" prevents a lot of telephone "ping pong." "I'll have him call you between 3:00 and 3:30" usually results in your party being there when you call. There are standard telephone message forms. Make sure they're used. You should know what the call is about, as well as the basic information such as name, affiliation, and phone number.

Don't make exceptions for long distance calls. Many administrators will jump at the announcement "It's long distance for you." So what? The likelihood of it being important is no greater than if the call had originated next door. Have it handled like all the rest. Your secretary should respond with the usual "I'm sorry, he's in a meeting right now. Can I help you?" The cost of the callback, if necessary, is normally less than the value of the protected time.

Take the time to explain to your secretary exactly how you want your messages recorded. Insist on having the caller's name spelled out if it is unfamiliar. Have the number and other information repeated back to the caller to ensure its accuracy. Emphasize the importance of taking the time to obtain relevant information, including how long the caller will be at the number. It is time well spent.

Some secretaries use the "Telephone & Visitors Log" to take messages. All the relevant information, such as name, number, date, and purpose of call is noted in the appropriate section, with the "Please call after 3 p.m." notation in the action section. The administrator receiving this form slips it into his or her "Personal Organizer," returns the call, and notes any further action necessary. There is no need to transfer information from a standard message form to the "Telephone & Visitors Log."

Not everyone agrees that calls should be screened. Negotiation authority Roger Dawson claims it is frequently faster to take calls, excusing yourself quickly, rather than have callbacks as a result of the secretary taking the calls. He suggests a reply such as "Hi, Jack. I'm busy right now. Can I call you back—or do you have a quick question?" Dawson claims the caller will opt for the quick question, sidestepping the usual social amenities and chitchat, reducing the length of the call to a minimum.

I suggest you experiment yourself, but my own opinion is that you should at least have your calls intercepted at certain times of the day when you are working on your priority projects. The time taken by five interruptions to your train of thought is usually much greater than the time taken for five callbacks immediately after the "quiet hour." And by having your secretary take the calls, you should find that some calls never reach you. Frequently people ask for you simply because you were the one who gave them your business card, or talked to them last. What they really might be calling about is information they think you can supply, not necessarily to talk to you personally.

You must also be careful that by taking your own calls and, due to time constraints, being abrupt, you don't leave the impression that you're giving everyone the brush-off. It's frequently better to call back later when you're not under so much pressure.

If you're going to be effective as an administrator you must not let yourself be victimized by the telephone. Don't let its facade of urgency fool you. Probably less than 20% of your calls could be classified as urgent. And, of those, over half could probably be directed to someone else.

If you absolutely refuse to have your calls intercepted, at least have your secretary advise the caller "He's busy right now. Shall I interrupt him?" Unless it is an emergency, most callers will decline the offer. They generally have more respect for your time than *you* do. Alternatively, you can supply your secretary with a list of people who should be put through regardless, with everyone else being intercepted. But be careful of this one. Important people can make unimportant requests.

When your quiet hour is over, be sure to return those calls that could not be handled by someone else. Respect for your own time should never be confused with lack of respect for the time of others. ***Make those calls yourself.*** It may save a little time by having your secretary make your calls for you and then hand the party over to you once they've been contacted. But it's doubtful, considering that you had to take the time to tell your secretary who to contact in the first place. And any time saving on your part is definitely at the expense of the *other party* because he or she is kept waiting on the line. Then what you're really communicating to the other person is that your time is more important than his or hers. Maybe your time *is* more important. And maybe you don't mind communicating it. But at least be aware of the possible consequences. We save time in order to increase our *total* effectiveness. We don't want to lose effectiveness in another area as a result of time saving.

When you are returning someone's call, tell this to the person who answers. The secretary may have been asked to screen the calls, causing a delay in the call being put through. Always announce your name and the purpose of your call. If the person is not available at that moment, get the name of the person you are talking to and tell that person where and when you can be reached. It is now the responsibility of the originator of the call to reach you—but make it as easy as possible. Make notes in your telephone log so you have a record of this attempt to return the call.

DON'T LET YOUR TELEPHONE BECOME A TIME WASTER

According to an article by Leon Fletcher, in the October 1982 issue of *The Toastmaster* ("How to Use Your Phone Better"), more than 250 billion phone calls are made each year in the U.S. alone—more than 1,000 calls a year for every man, woman and child in the nation. Have you ever considered the total time that could be saved if all those calls were reduced in length by only one minute each? Of course, we can't control other people's calls. But if we reduced our own 1000 calls by one minute, we would save the equivalent of over two full work-days each year. A minute is important when there are so many of them!

A newspaper article stated that in the U.S. alone, over 46 million telephones have been installed, an increase of over 10 million during the past decade. Is this increase in telephones and telephone usage good or bad? It depends on how they are used.

Everyone seems to be an avid telephone user. And rightly so, since phones are real time savers, eliminating the necessity of personal meetings, reams of paper, and missed deadlines.

The problem is the way phones are used. We sometimes discuss things on the telephone even though we will be seeing that person an hour later. We tend to socialize excessively, drag out conversations, call the same person several times in the day, interrupt calls rudely when someone walks into the office, half-listen while we fiddle with other jobs, fail to make notes, and forget to follow up on those items that are discussed. We sometimes make spontaneous calls without planning, ignore the phone while it rings incessantly, neglect to have calls intercepted, ignore the timesaving features of our telephone system, fail to make appointments for callbacks, and make no attempt to find out the best time of the day to call someone.

In general, people do not make effective use of the telephone. The simple process of planning outgoing calls and capturing information on a structured form such as the "Telephone & Visitors Log," described earlier, combined with efficient telephone techniques, could virtually cut telephone time in half and save U.S. organizations millions of dollars. The obvious savings would result from less time spent, as well as reduced long distance charges. But, equally important, would be improved communications, interpersonal relationships, and image in the community.

Your telephone does not have to be a time waster. Managed properly, it could slice an hour or more from your day.

THE BEST TIME TO CALL

Some people are always "tied up" or "in a meeting" first thing in the morning. Others are unavailable in the late afternoon. Some may be reached easily between 11 a.m. and noon. It varies with the individual, because everyone doesn't schedule their time the same way.

In some cases, a person may *always* be unavailable, since they have all their calls screened.

According to telephone consultant Harry Newton of Telecom Library Inc. (reported in the article "Put Time On Your Side" by Harold M. Emanuel in the October 1982 issue of *Management World*), only 22% of business calls are completed.

Time is frequently wasted in attempting to get in touch with people and "primetime" for telephone calls varies. So make a point of finding out the best time to call people, and record that information along with their names in your telephone directory. Don't be afraid to ask. A simple "What's the best time of the day to get hold of you, Charlie?" may result in some valuable information. Charlie may tell you he's always out of the office on Mondays, or is always tied up in the morning before 10 a.m., or usually uses the lunch hour to return calls.

Similar information may be available from the person's secretary. So if you fail to reach someone on your first attempt, always ask the secretary for the best time to call back. If you want the other person to call you back, make sure you tell the secretary when *you* can be reached as well.

Always be aware of how you waste other people's time. Don't insist on the party calling you back personally if you can get the information from somebody else. Always announce who's calling. And if you do leave a message, always leave your phone number as well. Don't force the other person to look it up. A brief statement as to what the call is about would also help the person be prepared when making the callback.

If you encounter voice mail when you call, and two-way communication is not necessary, leave your entire message and indicate that a callback is not required unless the person needs clarification.

TELEPHONE COURTESY

Whether you or someone else is answering the telephone, pick it up on the first ring. The tendency is to let the phone ring two or three times before answering it. Why? Because we want to finish what we are doing? If so, the next time you delay answering a telephone, ask yourself how much more you have actually accomplished. Chances are, the second that phone rings, you are distracted; your mind is now on the phone and not on your work. Delaying picking it up is simply a waste of time. On the other hand, picking it up on the first ring shows respect for the other person's time, impresses them with your promptness and business-like manner, and gets the call over with faster so you can resume your task.

Don't put a caller on hold before you at least give them a chance to say a few words. Nothing is more annoying than to have a call answered with "Jackson High, one minute, please," followed by silence or music. If you can afford the time to *answer* the phone you can afford a few extra seconds to let the callers introduce themselves before explaining that you have to put them on hold for a minute.

Similarly, if you are talking on the telephone and another telephone rings, provide more than an abrupt "Just a minute, please" before switching to the other caller. You have time for a brief but courteous explanation before the other phone rings three times. "I'm sorry. The other phone is ringing. Do you mind if I leave you for a moment to get their name and number?" Time being courteous is time well spent.

Many of the ideas discussed here involve making your telephone calls more efficient. But never become efficient at the expense of being effective. You are effective when you recognize the value of a student, parent, friend, or any human being. The callers are important—so treat them accordingly. And remember that angry callers are not angry at you, so don't take it personally. Letting them blow off a little steam may defuse a bomb.

Spending a little time on the telephone is usually a good investment of time. And though a practical suggestion is to work on routine items while listening, never sacrifice your power of concentration for a few trivial items on your "To Do" list. The call comes first. Many people cannot listen properly while doing "filler" work.

Chapter 7

Organizing Your Desk And Office

A TIME SAVING ENVIRONMENT

The location, layout, and condition of your office have an impact on how effectively you manage your time. Have you ever visited Caesar's Palace in Las Vegas? The environment there actually *encourages* you to spend time and money. Moving sidewalks take you inside (but leaving isn't as convenient). You must pass the gambling casino in order to get to the registration desk. After registering you have to wind your way through the gaming tables to get to the elevators. You're tempted. And when you start to gamble, it's so easy to continue. The drinks are free. The chairs are comfortable. Air conditioning and loud colors keep you from getting drowsy. There are no clocks on the walls. No windows. You lose track of time. The dealers payoff in larger denomination chips. You lose more and faster. The chips are only negotiable at Caesar's so you can't readily move to another casino. It's easy to buy chips at any table—but you have to find the casino cashier if you want to cash them in. Everything is conducive to the spending of time and money.

Take a lesson from Caesar's Palace. Develop an office environment that encourages the *saving* of time—and money. If you can influence the layout of the office do so. Arrange the desks to coincide with the work flow. Place office equipment so as to minimize steps, while keeping in mind the possible distractions. Decentralize storage cabinets so everyone's supplies are close at hand. If you need a centralized storage room, make sure it's easy to locate the various supplies. You might try painting the shelves in the supply cupboard different colors. All stationery, letterhead, forms, and paper products could be kept on the green shelf; all typewriter and other office equipment supplies on the red shelf; all small office supplies such as paperclips, rubber bands, staples, etc., on the blue shelf—and so on. Everyone would soon get to know they could find the timetables on the green shelf and the correction fluid on the red shelf, and it would make it easier to tell new staff members and visitors where to find something. Don't skimp on inexpensive equipment. Everyone should have their own stapler, 3-hole punch, pencil sharpener or whatever items they use frequently.

Don't run out of supplies or stationery. Organize the storage so there's a place for everything. Insist on everything being kept that way. For forms, letterhead, envelopes, promotion material, tape a copy to the outside of the box for easy identification. Number the cartons 1, 2, 3, etc., when they come in. Stack them in reverse order and when you get down to 2, reorder.

Have written procedures for all tasks. Have the staff members who are responsible for the tasks make up the procedures. Review them. Refine them. Simplify them if possible. And make everyone in the building aware of them.

Get a large wall calendar. Record all meetings, conferences, workshops, vacations, important deadlines, so everyone can see them.

Make sure your private office is arranged so as to attract a minimum of interruptions. Don't face the open doorway. Have your desk to one side, so people will have to go out of their way to see you. Or have your desk facing away from the doorway. If they are able to catch your eye from outside the office they will be tempted to walk inside and strike up a conversation. For the same reason, avoid having gathering spots outside your office such as coffee or duplicating equipment. One individual reported that the coffee maker was right outside his office door and people would kill time while the water boiled by walking into his office and socializing.

Have your office decorated tastefully, but simply. A lot of family photos, trophies, diplomas, certificates, and citations will encourage chitchat. Don't have ashtrays if you don't smoke. Or comfortable sofas if you don't sleep in your office. But plants are great, even if you don't garden. And a clock is a great reminder of the speed at which time passes—place it where your *visitor* can see it.

Arrange your working tools and furniture closely around your desk area. Don't place frequently used filing cabinets or bookcases on the other side of the room. You should have everything at your fingertips.

Your desk does not have to be large, but you must have sufficient working area. The desk is not meant for storage, so keep it clear of paperwork except for projects you are working on. Other projects should be retained in a follow-up file; the bulkier ones can be kept in colored manila folders, clearly identified. These should be kept in hanging files in your desk drawer. If your desk doesn't have a drawer large enough to hold files, I recommend you get one that does. If this is impossible, keep the follow-up file system and project files in a vertical file holder on the top of your desk or in a filing cabinet to the side of your desk.

Your office should be arranged so that everything is readily accessible. Every time you have to walk somewhere for supplies, you risk an extended interruption. So anticipate the envelopes, letterheads, pads, etc., which you will need, and include them in your inventory. If you need an extra cabinet or shelf on the wall near your desk, get one. Have a set of stacking trays on your desk or credenza bearing the names of the people who report to you, or whom you communicate with on a regular basis. This could include your assistant principal. Whenever there is something requiring their atten tion, jot notes on it and toss it in one of those trays. Invariably, they will interrupt you at least once every day and they can empty their tray when they do. Don't deliver mail to anyone who will be dropping in. Save yourself some trips.

Don't let your office environment control you. You spend too many hours there to suffer unnecessary inconveniences. If a floor receptacle prevents you from placing your desk where you want it, have it removed. If the door is in the wrong place, change it. If the lighting is poor, add more lights. If the rollers on your chair are worn, replace them. Any costs incurred are one-time costs; the time savings are forever. Experiment with several arrangements until you get the one that works best for you.

Couches are too comfortable and encourage socializing, but chairs placed around a conference table encourage results. Move the telephone so you have your back to the door when using it. This removes the temptation to be distracted by anyone walking into your office. You can't pay attention to two people at the same time.

THE FOLLOW-UP FILE

A clear desk does not guarantee that you'll be organized. But it helps. If you have a handful of material relating to a project and nowhere to put it, don't leave it on your desk or toss it back into the in-basket. Develop a follow-up file. This follow-up file is exclusive of your secretary's. If your secretary keeps a follow-up file and uses it to jog your memory or return letters, reports, etc., to you for follow-up or approval, that's great. But this is *your* personal follow-up file which contains the backup material for those tasks that you have scheduled in your time planner. Place paperwork into this follow-up file when a time to complete it has been blocked in your planning calendar.

The follow-up file system consists of 13 hanging files marked January, February, etc., and the last one marked "next year." One set of manila folders marked from 1 to 31, corresponding to the days of the month, is placed in the current month's hanging folder. (*See* Exhibit 7.) If it's the first of the month and you have emptied the day's project papers, move the manila folder to the next month's hanging folder.

This follow-up file system is simply an adjunct to your time planner. Your planner contains your work plan. When you arrive in the morning, flip open your time planner, and if you see a report scheduled for 9:00 a.m., you know exactly where to look for the backup papers needed—in that day's follow-up file.

If *more* papers are received related to a specific task that is scheduled for a future date, it's a simple matter to find the appropriate follow-up file folder. Simply flip through your time planner to find the date on which that project is scheduled.

For ongoing projects such as committee meetings, book manuscripts, and master class schedules, it's not necessary (or advisable) to jam all the backup material into the follow-up folders. Instead, use a colored manila folder bearing the project's name or title. Keep them in your right-hand desk drawer, along with your follow-up file. Use hanging folders for these project files for easy retrieval. You will soon know that the red folder is "A" project, the green folder the "B" project, and so on.

KEEP A CLEAR DESK

Once you have cleared your desk and scheduled the jobs you didn't have to do right away, you're well on your way to being organized. A few hours invested in this initial cleanup will save millions of precious minutes in the future. You will have eliminated some time wasters—shuffling papers, searching for things, distractions, working on trivial items. While you've got the momentum, do a good job of this initial cleanup. Empty those desk drawers, that shelf under your desk, those cluttered bookcases, credenza and filing cabinets.

Muster up enough courage to throw out anything you can't see an immediate use for. Have a place for everything and put everything in its place, within reason. But leave yourself the luxury of one junk drawer for all those U.F.O.'s (unidentified funny objects) you have collected, such as gold plated paper-clips, unusual business cards, and your sons' handcarved

"Follow-up" File System

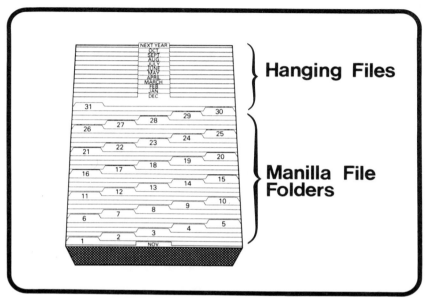

Hanging Files

Manilla File Folders

EXHIBIT 7
Follow-up File

thumbtack holder. You can carry the organization bit a little too far.

No administrator can do without that single junk drawer. We all need some disorganization somewhere in our lives. And sorting through that junk drawer every six months or so is more fun and more stress-relieving than an executive sandbox.

Once you have cleared your desk and emptied your in-basket, don't dump things back in again. People are tempted to use it as a holding basket for everything pending or puzzling. Don't. The trivial items will obscure the important ones, which soon become urgent. Fight procrastination by looking at it as an *action* basket.

You may be tempted to leave material on your desk temporarily, until you have a chance to work on it. Don't. You'll soon have so much temporary storage, it will become permanent clutter. You'll waste time searching for things. The minutes add up to hours. All those unfinished tasks scattered before you will produce anxiety and stress. You'll be tempted to hop from one unfinished job to another. You'll have difficulty concentrating on the task at hand. Messy desks decrease effectiveness. After all, who can plan with all those urgent, unfinished tasks taunting them? A clear desk will give you a psychological lift. You'll look organized, you'll feel organized, and you will *be* organized.

An integral part of your organized work area is your filing system. In spite of the "if in doubt, throw it out" policy, you will have paperwork that you must keep. So you need more than a follow-up file, idea file, and project files.

PERSONALIZE YOUR FILING SYSTEM

File your material so it's easy to retrieve. If you feel you will never need to retrieve it, scrap it. Use hanging folders appropriately labeled. Store them in similarly labeled manila folders so you will always return the folder to the right spot (your hanging folders need never leave the drawer or cabinet). You could file alphabetically according to category, *e.g.,* Suppliers, A to Z; Administration, A to Z; Buildings and Equipment, A to Z; etc.

Articles, job descriptions, newsletters, bulletins, and anything else you refer to frequently could be kept in 3-ring binders. Label them clearly for easy identification. Have a binder for each of the regular meetings held each month (*i.e.,* curriculum council, administration/union or liaison committee, child study team, etc.) Place agendas and relevant information in the appropriate binder *as they are received*. You can review the information prior to the meeting. Purge your files regularly; resist the urge to buy more filing cabinets.

Brief clippings from newspapers and magazines, one-liners, ideas, could be stuck onto 3" × 5" index cards with a glue stick and filed according to category. You could tie the various files together with a central reference card file. For example, if you arbitrarily assign a number to every piece of paper you file, you could enter this number in the reference file at the same time. This reference file could be categorized by topic, name, etc. If the budget can afford it, you might consider purchasing a personal computer to simplify cross-referencing.

If you read something that you will want to use later, it's generally a good idea to photocopy that page, or write out the idea on a card and file it under the appropriate category. Alternatively, you could jot down the book and page number on an index card and file that in the appropriate spot.

THE ALPHANUMERICAL FILE

A simple filing system that eliminates misfiling, makes retrieval easy, and assures that something retrieved from the files is put back in the same spot again, is the alphanumerical system. Here, each category has a reference file folder containing a listing of all subheadings within that category. Each subheading is assigned a number, and that number only, not the heading, is marked on the file folders within that category. *See* Exhibit 8.

For example, assume you have a category titled "Media." Take a folder, mark the tab with the word "Media," and inside that folder tape an 8½" × 11" sheet of lined paper and head it up "Media." Under this heading, list all the subcategories or subheadings that you need. Don't bother listing them alphabetically. It's easy to glance down the list later to find the subheading you are looking for, as long as the list doesn't go beyond one page in length.

Now assign a number series to this "Media" category. If it's "100," mark "100" opposite the word "Media" on the index tab of the main reference file folder. Then opposite the subheadings, assign numbers 101, 102, 103, etc. Next, mark these numbers on a set of file folders, and file the papers in these folders, marking the same number on each piece of paper you file.

For example, if one of your subheadings is "Television" and it had been assigned the number "106," you would mark "106" on the piece of paper to be filed there. When you want to

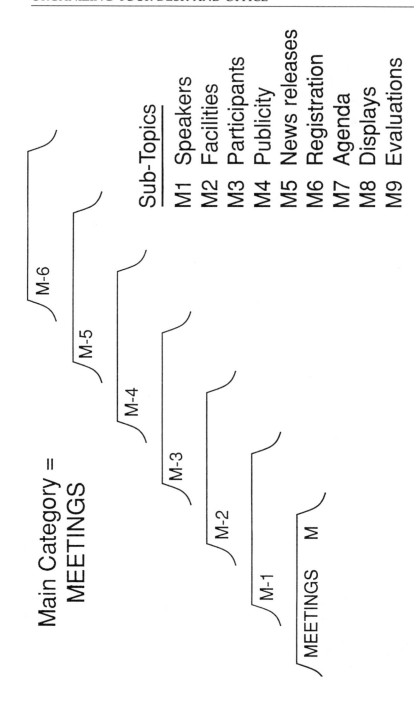

EXHIBIT 8
Alphanumerical File System

retrieve it from the file later, turn to the reference file folders, glance down the list until you see "Television," note the number opposite it, and pull out the appropriate folder. To re-file, simply stick it in the folder bearing the same number that appears on the piece of paper. Misfiling is unlikely, even when dozens of people are using the same files.

With this system it is easy to add, eliminate, or combine categories. Since no titles appear on the individual folders, it is easy to use the numbered folders for other subcategories if the existing subcategory is eliminated. For a detailed discussion of this system refer to the book *File, Don't Pile* by Pat Dorff (St. Martin's Press: New York, NY, 1986).

The more time spent in filing a piece of correspondence, the less time spent in retrieval. But how often do you have to retrieve something from the files? It may be more economical and faster to set up a simple system based on topic or date. One secretary insists that filing by date is faster—even for retrieval. She claims her boss is always asking for a letter that he received "about a month ago" or "last January or February." So she has labeled the folders by the month, regardless of the topic or person originating the letter. Set up a system that satisfies *your* needs. And remember, the name of the game is retrieval, not storage.

If it's your secretary that does the actual filing, make it as easy as possible for him or her. If it's your memo, letter or report, you probably know where it should be filed. So jot down this information at the top of the paper. Also, the throw-out date, if you don't plan to keep it forever. If it has to be followed up later, note the follow-up date so the secretary can stick it in the follow-up file under the appropriate date. It's easier to jot a few words on each piece of paper than to have the secretary guess at what to do with it.

YOUR PERSONAL ORGANIZER

The two previous chapters described the Delegation Record and Telephone Log. Put these forms in a binder, add other forms and information as required, and you have your own personal organizer. Keep it on your desk, toss it in your briefcase when you travel, and you have relevant information at your fingertips.

One form you might add to your "Personal Organizer" is a **Telephone Directory** (*see* Exhibit 9). Don't keep business cards which accumulate in desk drawers, produce clutter, and waste time when you're searching for a number. By adding a set of alphabetical tabs to your binder you can include as many sheets as you want under the various alphabetical headings. If the directory becomes outdated you only have to copy over one page at a time.

By having your telephone directory in the same binder as your telephone log forms, it's easy to immediately transfer new numbers into your directory when you get them from your callers.

When you enter the name of a new acquaintance, use the "Information" section to record something about that person. This serves as a memory key or reminder so you'll recall who that person is several months (or years) later. For example, a simple "met at State Conference," "friend of Sue Black" or "new principal at Sycamore Elementary School" will immediately identify the person for you through association. You might also use this space to note other information about the person, *e.g.*, name of her assistant principal, her favorite food, best time to reach her, etc.

The Telephone Directory forms should also have space for Fax numbers as well as the usual "Home" and "Business" numbers.

Keep plenty of notepaper in your personal organizer so you can capture information when interviewing students, staff, teachers or parents. Get in the habit of writing things down. Relying on your memory may not only waste time, but cause serious problems as well.

You can make up your own organizer or purchase one of the dozens available in office supply stores. Keep it simple; you don't want to spend so much time keeping organized that you don't have time to do the work! The forms shown in these chapters, as well as the time planner, were designed for my own use. They are available from Harold Taylor Time Consultants Inc., 6860 Gulfport Blvd. S., Suite 330, Gulfport, Fl 33707 (1-800-361-8463).

TELEPHONE DIRECTORY

NAME — COMPANY — ADDRESS	DESCRIPTION	TELEPHONE NUMBERS
		Business: .... Home: ....
		Business: .... Home: ....
		Business: .... Home: ....
		Business: .... Home: ....
		Business: .... Home: ....
		Business: .... Home: ....
		Business: .... Home: ....
		Business: .... Home: ....
		Business: .... Home: ....
		Business: .... Home: ....

EXHIBIT 9
Telephone Directory

Chapter 8

Coping With The Paperwork

GETTING RID OF THE BACKLOG

Do you find yourself buried in paperwork, magazines, and junk mail, with an overflowing in-basket and a desk drawer crammed with files, reports and trivia? Do you have stacks of material on your credenza, window ledges and filing cabinets? Then you may have difficulty coping with current material. You must first get rid of the backlog, and organize yourself so the paperwork will never get ahead of you again.

But first you must clean up your desk, office, and files. Here is a 10-point system for the initial cleanup so you can stay on top of your paperwork:

- Block a three-hour period in your planning calendar. If it's impossible during working hours, schedule it at night or on a weekend.

- Empty all desk drawers, ledges, etc., of paperwork. Don't tackle filing cabinets at this stage—only your desk, credenza, and any visible piles of paperwork.

* Toss all paperwork into three envelope boxes marked "Priority," "Routine," and "Junk Mail." Stack the magazines separately.

* As you carry out the previous step, quickly scan the material and toss out the obvious garbage.

* One of the desk drawers should be a file drawer. If not, use a file cabinet drawer that is within reach of your desk. Install hanging folders.

* Use 13 of the hanging folders for a follow-up file as described earlier. Label the other folders with titles of your major ongoing projects. Every hanging file should contain a similarly labeled manila file folder.

* One or more of your desk drawers will contain "non-paperwork"—miscellaneous paraphernalia and office supplies. Separate those items you actually *use* on a regular basis, and organize them in an organizer tray. Retain in a shallow drawer.

* Throw out whatever items your willpower will allow. Place the other items in a shoebox; label it "Junk Drawer," along with the year, and stash it away in some dark closet. If you haven't missed anything by the time you discover the shoebox again, scrap it.

* Go through those envelope boxes, starting with the one labeled "Priority," dealing with each piece of paper as you pick it up. Scrap it, delegate it, do it, or schedule a time to do it later. In the latter case, block off time to do it in your planner, and put the paperwork in the appropriate follow-up file.

* It is unlikely you will be able to dispense with all of the paperwork in 3 hours. Set the boxes aside and dedicate at least a half hour every morning to systematically going through this paperwork until it is all scrapped, done, delegated, or scheduled for a later time. In the meantime, keep on top of the incoming mail so another backlog isn't created. We'll discuss how a little later.

Parkinson's Law is normally quoted in reference to activities expanding to fill the time available for them. The solution: Set deadlines on all activities, meetings, and appointments—the thought being, that if we have less time available, we will work more efficiently as well as concentrate on priorities rather than trivia.

But Parkinson's Law refers to *things* as well. Clutter expands to fill the space available for it. Large desks accumulate more paperwork. Spacious offices generate more paraphernalia. And even large pencil caddies attract more pencils, pens, letter openers, markers, etc.—most of which are never used. Limit the amount of clutter by limiting the size of offices, desks, bookcases, cabinets, and yes, even pencil caddies. You don't need all that space. It simply encourages procrastination; it's easier to keep something than to throw it out or file it or give it away. Would you believe some people actually keep dry pens and broken pencils, if there's a handy spot to store them? By limiting space, you force yourself to store only the important things you know you will need. The less important ones will get tossed.

HANDLING INCOMING MAIL

An in-basket that's never empty, stacks of paper on the desk, magazines piled on bookcases and credenzas, bulging file folders that make retrieval an adventure—these are some of the signs of poor mail handling.

If you want to keep on top of paperwork, eliminate excessive handling, shuffling, searching and storage, and experience the joy of an empty in-basket, here is what you need:

* One slim, shallow in-basket;

* A series of stacking trays, bearing the names of the people you assign tasks to;

* 3-ring binders to hold the most recent copies of documents that should be retained, such as financial statements, minutes of meetings, articles in a particular area of interest, etc.;

- A follow-up file consisting of monthly hanging folders and a set of 1 to 31 manila folders;

- A separate hanging folder marked "To Do" or "Pending" or whatever. Preferably all these folders will be in your desk drawer on hanging rails;

- A "permanent" file system that *you* can understand and use easily. This will probably be an alphabetical or alphanumerical system;

- A week-at-a-glance planning calendar complete with "to do" and daily follow-up sections, and days broken into at least half-hour segments (such as the Taylor Time Planner);

- The necessary office supplies at your fingertips: 3-hole punch, stapler, glue stick, index cards, red and black pens, paper clipper (for slicing out articles), post-it notes, self-adhesive colored labels, a "white-out" correction pen;

- A large wastebasket and recycling basket;

- Self-inking stamps with appropriate messages for quick replies, speedy memos, and business cards;

- Access to a photocopier, fax machine, telephone, and typist (if you don't do it yourself). A hand-held pocket recorder and transcribing equipment would be useful.

The above materials and equipment are spelled out because you must have the means to keep the paperwork flowing. If you have no place to put the paperwork or no way to handle it immediately, it will accumulate and form another backlog. There's nothing more depressing than an overwhelming backlog of paperwork and no time to work on it.

To keep on top of current incoming mail and to avoid adding to that backlog, here's a procedure you might adopt:

- Choose a definite time period each day—say a half-hour every morning—to dispense with the previous day's mail. Don't vary the time, always allow that half-hour or more—and *ignore* the mail until it's time to work on it. Move your in-basket away from your desk if the temptation to peek is too great.

• When you pick up the top piece of mail, don't put it back or drop it on your desk. Either do it, delegate it, scrap it, place it in your follow-up file for a scheduled time to do it, or put it in that "To Do" file to be worked on during the week.

• Treat this mail time as a "quiet hour." Have calls and visitors intercepted if possible during this period of time. Close your office door if you have one, avoid distractions, and don't leave your desk during this period. There could be a myriad of letters, reports, magazines, meeting notices, "junk mail" items and other paperwork in that in-basket each day. The "mail-time" is a work session as well as a planning session in which you sort, discard, do, file, prioritize and schedule. Afterwards, the in-basket should be empty. Here's how each item you pick up might be handled:

1. *A thank you letter from a textbook salesperson.* Scrap it. Other candidates for the recycle basket might be unsolicited newsletters, subscription requests, promotional letters, copies of original letters meant to keep you informed. Be ruthless. "When in doubt, throw it out" is a good motto.

2. *A folder from an organization such as the American Association of School Administrators announcing a seminar that you would like to attend.* If it's important to attend, schedule it into your planner and register immediately. If you only plan to attend if nothing more important comes up on that day, toss it into your follow-up file for review a week before the session. Make a note in your planner to check the follow-up file on that day. Then pencil the seminar commitment into your planner so you won't book anything of *lesser* importance that day. If you *do* register for the seminar, mark the relevant

information into your planner on that date and *discard* the brochure, etc. Keep as little material as possible.

3. *A letter requesting a reply.* If you have the answer, respond immediately, using the fastest way possible, either

   a. by telephone (be sure to make notes in your telephone log);

   b. by writing your reply on the letter itself and keeping a copy only if necessary. (You could stamp the notation "In order to reply as promptly as possible, we've made marginal notes. Please excuse the informality.");

   c. by dictating or typing a reply.

   The point here is not to delay something that could be completed in a few minutes. If you want to justify a marginal note on letters from outside the school, fax the letter and reply back to the sender. They will be impressed with your sense of urgency.

4. *A request from the superintendent or a parent that is obviously a priority and must be completed by next week.* Schedule time in your planner early next week to work on it and put the paperwork in the follow-up file for that date.

   Any paperwork that is a priority (*i.e.,* relates to professional goals) should be scheduled the same as you would schedule time for an appointment. Don't toss important items back into the in-basket where they could be forgotten.

5. *A meeting notice for an upcoming curriculum council meeting.* If you plan to attend, mark it in your planner along with the relevant information (time, place, etc.) and scrap the notice. If there is an agenda or report to be taken to the meeting, put them in the follow-up file or in the appropriate meeting binder.

6. *A professional magazine, such as "Educational Leadership."* Assuming it's one you want to look at, scan the contents page, tear or cut out the articles of interest, and toss out the magazine. Or if the mag-

azine has to be circulated, have the marked articles photocopied. The loose articles can be retained in a"reading file" kept in your briefcase for use during idle time—such as long waits in doctors' offices or airplanes, etc.

7. *A newspaper.* If it's a paper relevant to your job and necessary to review, flip through it quickly, cutting out those articles you want to read. Alternatively, you can rip out the entire page on which the article appears. The point is to reduce bulk and get the information into a folder where it can be easily dispensed with later. Thinner publications, such as "Better Teaching" newsletters, can be retained intact and placed in your reading file.

8. *Minutes of a liaison committee meeting.* If there is no action to be taken on your part, immediately file it in a 3-ring binder, appropriately identified. At the same time, toss out the oldest minutes. Keep only the last 12 issues or so—unless you're responsible for retaining the only complete set in the building.

9. *Letters, requests, etc., from parents, teachers, students, that are not priorities and which you cannot complete in the time you have left.* Record them on your "Things To Do" list in the time planner and toss any related paperwork into your "To Do" file folder. Only *priority* tasks should be scheduled in a particular time slot in your planner.

10. *Paperwork involving tasks that could be completed by others.* Assign them immediately, marking a due date on them and tossing them into the appropriate out-basket (one of those stacking trays). Make a notation in the "follow-up" section of the time planner (preferably in red so it stands out) on the day that you have requested it be completed. Delegate everything possible, always assign a realistic due date, and make a note of that due date for follow-up.

11. *Green sheets, requisitions, early dismissal requests, personal leave requests all requiring your approval.* Initial and move on. Anything that can be done quickly, do it. Don't toss it aside until later.

12. *Telephone message slips from people trying to reach you.* Unless an obvious emergency, leave them until *after* your mail. Or phone just before lunch to keep conversations brief. Stick them on the phone, or on a "spike" near the phone.

13. *Brochures and catalogs from National Education Association, video resource companies, book publishers, etc.* If you have no immediate need for materials, jot the title of the catalog and source in your Personal Organizer before scrapping the catalogs. You can always ask for one if there's a need later. Alternatively, pass them on to your secretary for filing.

14. *Information pamphlets and booklets on Earth Day, At Risk Kids, Controlling Sexual Harassment in Schools—that you want to read.* Unless the need is this instant, toss them in your reading file along with the magazine articles, newsletters and newspaper clippings.

There are hundreds of types of paperwork items possible. The point is not to toss them back into your in-basket or on your desk where they will be repeatedly handled, delayed or misplaced. Items to be filed should be filed immediately. Business cards should be scrapped after recording essential information into your directory. Keep only what is necessary. Remove paperclips and substitute staples instead. Keep the paperwork flowing and resist the urge to toss it back into the basket. If you need more time to dispense with your mail, you might want to schedule another session right after lunch. The "do it now" habit is important when it comes to keeping your in-basket clear and preventing another backlog.

FILING MADE EASY

Frequently we have odd-sized mailers, cards, newspaper clippings, etc., which are awkward to file or retrieve. Here are some suggestions for making them readily accessible.

Magazine articles. These could be 3-hole punched and filed in 3-ring binders. Have a separate binder for every major topic. If you have only a few articles on each of many topics, use one binder, but have a separate section with divider and tab for each topic. Remember when filing anything, the objective is to make it easy to retrieve later. If you feel you will never refer to it again, don't file it.

Newspaper clippings. Seldom are we fortunate enough to have newspaper articles appear in an 8½" × 11" format. But if they are *smaller*, simply paste them onto 8½" × 11" paper so they can be filed in those 3-ring binders (or into hanging files if that's your preference). Don't toss them into files where they become lost or fall out whenever you take out the file. And don't 3-hole punch them, because they will invariably tear out after the binder is opened a few times—photocopy them first.

Oversized clippings can be cut to size by slicing off columns and pasting them onto a second sheet. Or, if they're simply too long or too wide, paste the bulk of the article to the 8½" × 11" sheet and simply fold the overlap. Photocopying the article first will also prevent fading. A few minutes spent filing will pay dividends later.

Ideas, one-liners, quotes. Sometimes we may want to make a note of a new product, humorous saying, poem, quote, joke, etc. Index cards are good for this. Simply write, type, or paste the idea on a 3" × 5" or 5" × 7" index card and categorize the cards in a file box. I kept hundreds of time management ideas categorized under different headings such as meetings, paperwork, telephone, etc., with this method. You could use a computer for items that have to be typed or written.

Newsletters, bulletins. Three-ring binders are ideal for newsletters, bulletins, minutes of meetings, budgets, etc. They can be filed with the current one in front, and as the binder gets full, discard the older ones at the back. With file folders or hanging files, people have a tendency to keep on filing and never purging. Binders, like self-cleaning ovens, are easily kept neat and clean.

Letters, reports. Normal correspondence is usually kept in an alphabetical file system. Use hanging folders in which to place those manila folders. Don't allow paperclips into the file system—they cause nothing but grief. Marking the "throw out date" on letters as they are filed makes later purging easier. An alternative is the alphanumerical system in which the files are broken down into categories and all the folders (other than the main category folder) bear numbers instead of topics.

Forms, requisitions, notices. If you have quantities of form letters, notices, letterheads, etc., which you use on an ongoing basis, keep them in an open storage unit with individual cubicles so they're easily accessible. Don't store them in files or vertical dividers or the forms will become permanently warped. Store them flat, and mark each compartment so each form has its individual slot. Always take the time to return extra copies to their designated spot. Rushing any filing operation wastes time later. People seldom complain about the time it takes to put things away, but most people complain about the time it takes to *find* something.

Active mail, follow-up letters. A follow-up file system, a pending file, or stacking trays should solve the problem of where to house those items being processed.

There are many ways of filing material, from chronological files to microfiche and computers. You should choose the simplest method that will serve your particular situation. Take a look at the types of material that you must keep for future reference and then select the system that will make retrieval easy. If you think you may never need to look at something again, don't file it, toss it. But never put something in an unlikely spot thinking you'll remember where you put it. Chances are you will forget within a few days. But if you file things in an orderly, structured way that makes sense, you will know where to look for it when you need it. The more time you spend on developing a foolproof file system, the easier things will be to retrieve in the future.

DON'T BE A PAPERWORK PACKRAT

Most people are guilty of filing too much. If the item is available elsewhere, consider throwing out your copy. It's convenient to have everything at your fingertips, but not logical if you only refer to it once a year. Old copies of newsletters, minutes of meetings, budgets, reports, etc., are seldom looked at again.

How much better if only *one* person retained a complete set instead of everyone on the mailing list!

If you have several binders containing certain reports or bulletins, throw out everything beyond 12 months. When your new copy arrives, toss out the oldest copy when you file the newest addition. It's usually only the last few issues that you have to refer to again. If your experience is that you never refer to *any* back issues, why keep anything? Take action on the current one, and then scrap it.

If you receive copies of letters directed to someone else, it's probably safe to scrap it once you've noted the contents. Even letters directed to *you* will be filed by the originator so most of them could be scrapped after the action has been taken. You'll know the exceptions. Keep as little unsolicited material (junk mail) as possible. If you have to keep it, thin it out first and staple together only those items that will be used or referred to later. Many faxes are followed up by the original, so scrap the fax copy as soon as you receive the original. More and more "junk faxes" are being sent. Don't fall into the trap of keeping them because you think someone might have requested the material be sent to you. Also, get rid of those glossy but useless premiums or promotional items you receive, those unsolicited magazines, business cards—and, oh yes, who needs 21 calendars for next year!

Chapter 9

Effective Delegation

WORK SMARTER, NOT HARDER

Delegation by some school administrators is a real challenge due to contract constraints, assignment constraints and limited staff members. And yet delegation *can* take place, whether it is to assistant principals, secretaries, teachers, or others.

One school superintendent in Arkansas was accustomed to having the morning newspaper on his desk each morning when he arrived at 7:30. It would be placed there by a lady custodian who had the boring, routine job of keeping a few offices clean and tidy. She was a good worker, bright, loyal and, until then, unnoticed. The superintendent asked her if she would like to glance through the paper before putting it on his desk, highlighting all the education news. She accepted eagerly, her job became more meaningful, and the superintendent saved time by not having to read the entire paper to identify news relevant to his administrative position. The superintendent also remarked that she did a better job than he.

Delegation ranges from minor assignments, such as the one above, to major decision-making that impacts upon the success of a program or the reputation of a school. It is the process of sharing your job with others and holding those individuals responsible for the successful completion of the tasks assigned. You cannot hold anyone responsible for carrying out an assignment without also delegating the amount of authority needed to carry out the responsibility assigned. You cannot hold a person responsible for improving the appearance of a newsletter, for instance, without the authority to choose the typestyle, pick the colors and revise the layout. Nor can you assign the responsibility of organizing a staff luncheon without the authority to choose a menu and arrange the seating plan.

The more authority a staff member is given, the less involvement is required on the part of the administrator, and the greater the burden that is lifted from his/her shoulders. But the more authority a staff member has, the greater the impact that person has on the success of the school. Administrators must have confidence in the staff in order to risk delegating.

And it *is* a risk, since the administrator must shoulder the blame for a job poorly done even though it may be someone else's error. The ultimate responsibility still rests with the administrator.

Yet delegation is the greatest time saver available to educators at all levels. It frees time for more important tasks, allows you to plan more effectively and helps relieve the pressure of too many jobs, too many deadlines, and too little time. Delegation actually extends results from what you can do personally to what you can control. It is also the most effective way of developing staff members. When you are delegating, you are working smarter, not harder.

We have many reasons for not delegating. We don't have time to train others. They can't do it as well or as quickly as we can. We're afraid they might goof. But in many cases these reasons are simply excuses. Sure it will take time to train them. However, every hour invested now will bring you hundreds of free hours in the future. It's unlikely our staff members can do as good a job as we can. But how about when we started? We weren't always as good at our jobs as we are now. Be willing to accept less at first. As they become more experienced, the jobs will improve. They'll goof. Everyone makes mistakes. But that's the price we have to pay in order to free up our time, develop our staff members, and expand our effectiveness.

What jobs should we delegate? A good starting place is to list all the jobs we do on a recurring basis, no matter how small. They all take time. Then look for those jobs that take the biggest chunks of time. If they require little training, great. But if you must train, schedule time to do it. Perhaps a half hour each day or two hours each week. Set the time aside and stick to a regular schedule. Time you spend now will pay big dividends later.

Also, look at those jobs that don't take much time, but are repeated frequently. They usually require little training, and all those 10-minute increments add up in the course of a month or a year.

You won't want to delegate critical jobs that could endanger your position nor jobs that involve confidential information. But there are probably many jobs that someone else could do for you.

One of the roles of an administrator is that of a manager. Managers get things done through other people. A manager plans, organizes, staffs, directs, controls, innovates. But a manager does not get bogged down with jobs that someone else can do.

PRINCIPLES OF DELEGATION

Improper delegation is worse than no delegation at all. It not only creates a greater demand on your own time, but messes up your staff members' time as well. Be careful what you delegate, how you delegate, and to whom you delegate. Here are a few ground rules for effective delegation:

* *Don't delegate what you can eliminate.* If it's not important enough for you to do personally, it's probably not important enough for your people to do either. Respect their time and their ability. Don't waste it on nonpro-

ductive or unprofitable trivia. Your success can be multiplied a thousand times if you concentrate on the high-return jobs and encourage your people to do likewise—don't spoil it by using your staff as a dumping ground for "garbage" jobs.

* *Delegate the things you don't want to delegate.* We tend to hang on to the things we like doing, even when they interfere with more important tasks, and even though our subordinates could probably do them just as well. Share the interesting work with your staff. One of the most important advantages of effective delegation is the fact that it enriches your employees' jobs. Don't limit your delegation to the boring, repetitive tasks—look for the interesting ones as well.

* *Delegate—don't abdicate.* Dumping jobs onto your staff and then disappearing is not delegation—it's organizational suicide. Delegation must be planned. Consult with your staff members first; select people you think are capable of doing the job and would like to do the job. Train them. Delegate gradually, insist on feedback, and then leave them alone.

* *Delegate the objective, not the procedure.* One of the bonuses you receive from effective delegation is the fact that in many cases the job is done better in the hands of someone else. Don't resent it, encourage it. Delegate the whole task for specific results, de-emphasizing the actual procedure. Your staff members, under less pressure, less harried, and with a fresh viewpoint, will likely improve upon the method you've been using. Review results, not the manner in which he or she arrived at them!

* *Don't always delegate to the most capable people.* Delegation is one of the most effective methods of developing your people. Don't continually delegate to the most capable ones, or they'll get stronger, while the weak ones get weaker. Take the extra effort to spread delegation across the board to develop a strong team with no weak links.

• *Trust your staff.* Be sure to delegate the authority as well as the responsibility. Don't continually look over their shoulders, interfere with their methods, or jump on them when they make mistakes. Be prepared to trade short-term errors for long-term results. Maintain control without stifling initiative.

Henry Ford is claimed to have said "If anyone is indispensable, fire him." A little extreme perhaps; but it does get the message across that people who do not delegate actually impede an organization's progress. If you hog all the information to yourself and refuse to delegate, quite possibly you can't be replaced. But you can't be promoted either!

Rarely can an organization afford to risk its life by maintaining blockages. Sooner or later they must resort to surgery. One of the goals of every administrator should be to train someone else to replace him or her. Failure to do this blocks the possibility of promotion at all levels in the organization and stifles initiative. Do you have training of others and systematic delegation as one of the performance targets for some of the people reporting to you? If not, consider it.

ASSUME YOU HAVE AN EXCELLENT STAFF

You have probably heard about the experiment where average students were introduced to a teacher as handpicked, high-I.Q. students. The teacher was told that these particular students could be expected to show dramatic improvements over the course of the school year. And since the teacher expected great things from these "special" students, they received great things. The students improved remarkably.

It's the old self-fulfilling prophecy at work. Expect little and you'll get little; expect much and you'll get much. If you mentally label your staff as incompetent and not worth the time to train, they won't disappoint you. But if you approach them as though they were handpicked, high-I.Q. people who were capable of great achievements, you will have a completely different caliber of person on your staff.

If "stupid" people make an error it's obviously because they misinterpreted your instructions or weren't capable of carrying them out. But if "clever" people make an error, there's a possibility that you didn't explain it properly, or they met an unforeseeable roadblock.

Always assume you have "clever" staff members. And when things go wrong, look to yourself for the reason. Did you explain the situation properly? Did you rush through the instructions? Did you forget to warn the person about those exceptional circumstances that might occur? Did you mistakenly take certain prior knowledge for granted? Were your instructions ambiguous?

If you find yourself blameless, then there's only one possible answer: Even clever, superior staff members slip up once in a while. It might even have happened to you on occasion. So see it as it is—an honest error that could have happened to anyone. Don't get upset, point the blame, or berate the person. Nothing you can do now can turn back the clock and prevent the error from happening. It has already happened. But you *can* help prevent the same error from recurring. You *can* make it a learning experience for the staff member. And you *can* protect the person's self-esteem. How? By condemning the error, but not the person who made it.

Always give your people the benefit of the doubt. Few would make a mistake on purpose. And when they do make a mistake, their self-image suffers. What they need at this point is not your criticism, but your assurance. Help build up their self-confidence. Let them know that you're not blaming them for the mistake and that it could have happened to anyone. Then ask them if they have any suggestions as to "how we can reduce the chances of this happening again."

People learn from their mistakes. **What** they learn is up to you. They could learn that making a mistake is painful and demeaning and that they shouldn't take risks. Or they could learn that if they do make an error they should try to bury it so they don't get raked over the coals. However, they could learn that to err is human and the name of the game is to make as few mistakes as possible, to learn from the mistakes that do occur, and to continue to strive to be creative and innovative.

Assume your staff members are a handpicked group of clever, creative, dedicated individuals. Eventually you may prove yourself to be right.

UTILIZE YOUR SECRETARY'S TIME WISELY

The secretary is your most important delegatee. But he/she is already the dumping ground for a myriad of tasks and victim of countless interruptions. The desperate salesperson fighting the zero-budget routine, the harried parent dropping off Suzie's lunch, the irate mother convinced that a teacher is out to "get" her little Johnny. The secretary sits precariously in the line of fire. It is essential that you meet with him or her early in the day to discuss one another's schedules and set priorities. Make him/her a part of the management team. Provide the necessary time management tools and training. Delegate challenging and meaningful tasks and encourage him/her to suggest ways current procedures, tasks and reports could be eliminated, abbreviated or improved.

Don't be a perfectionist when managing your secretary. While it's important that such things as community correspondence be top quality, remember that by spending unnecessary time on a task, other high payoff activities may be short-changed.

Communicate. The more a secretary knows, the more he or she will be able to help you. A knowledgeable secretary can save you hours each week by providing information to callers and visitors without having to disturb you. When you attend a conference or take a vacation, spend some time briefing your secretary on matters that are likely to occur during your absence.

Above all, set a good example and show respect for your secretary's time. Plan your day. Accumulate the non-urgent requests instead of interrupting him/her frequently. Keep a folder to house assignments of lesser importance for later review. Place realistic deadlines on all tasks. Respect the secretary's time as well as your own.

Chapter 10

Streamlining Your Communications

TAKE TIME TO LISTEN

An ancient tribe of American Indians had a proverb "Listen, or thy tongue will keep thee deaf." In spite of all the books and seminars available on effective listening, few people take the trouble to really understand what a person is saying. Dale Galloway, in his book *Confidence Without Conceit*, points out that the more authority people get, the less they are forced to listen to others. And yet their need to listen is even greater, since they have to depend on others for their information.

Educators are busy. And the busier they get the less patience they seem to have when it comes to listening. It isn't easy to devote full attention to someone sitting in front of you. There is a tendency to mentally review what you just did or said at the assembly. Or reflect on the items you want to raise with the superintendent at the meeting concerning the teacher who is being denied tenure. There is so much to do and so little time. The important thing to remember is that listening does not waste time, it saves time. It's no wonder the *Bible* tells us that everyone should be "quick to listen, slow to speak, and slow to become angry." For anger and speaking frequently get us into trouble as well as consuming a lot of time. But how many times does listening to others get us into trouble? Listening is a critical part of the communication process. Ineffective listening can cause errors, misunderstandings, broken relationships, and even tragedies. Like planning, listening takes time initially, but frees up more time later by preventing time-consuming and costly crises from occurring.

Listening not only saves time, improves communications, and prevents errors, it also improves morale. Everyone likes to be heard. Being ignored is demeaning. It's even worse when someone pretends to listen while staring blankly through the person, thoughts on some other pressing problem. You can't fake it. You have to be genuinely interested in the person and what he or she is saying. It can't be rushed. "Haste makes waste" is as true for listening as it is for anything else. If you honestly don't have the time at that precise moment to really listen to someone, be honest with the person and with yourself and say so. Schedule a session later when you can devote adequate time to the process.

Listening is a skill that can be developed, according to John Drakeford, author of *The Awesome Power of Positive Attention* (Broadman Press, 1990). He suggests an acrostic on the word "listen" to remind us what the listening process is all about:

- *L*earn the truth about listening.

- *I*nvestigate the difference between hearing and listening.

- *S*how your interest in every way.

- *T*ame unruly emotions.

- *E*liminate side excursions.

- *N*ever interrupt.

The truth is that effective listening is not related to intelligence or the amount of reading we do. Nor is the skill developed automatically as we grow older. Hearing is not the same as listening. To quote Drakeford, "The word *hear* describes the process whereby a sound comes through the air to your ear, where it is changed to neural current and transmitted to the brain. The word *listening* is used for the process whereby we sort the messages and decide which stimulus will have our attention."

Showing your interest in every way refers to utilizing every part of your body—mouth, eyes, etc., to make the other person feel loved, valued and worthwhile. It is also important not to react emotionally to "red flag" words that could disrupt communications. And not to drift into other thoughts while the person is speaking. This is difficult, since the average person speaks at about 125 words per minute, while we can listen at 4 or 5 times that speed. With all this spare time to kill, our mind wanders, daydreams, takes little mental excursions and frequently doesn't get back to the speaker in time. We miss points, meanings. We guess, misinterpret. We can't slow down our thinking process, but we can utilize the spare time more effectively. The secret is to *stay with the speaker*. Review and mentally summarize what he has said. Listen between the lines, look for those nonverbal communications. Weigh the evidence being used to support his points. *But stick with him*. Don't drift into space or start formulating your own reply while he's still speaking.

Equally difficult is to avoid interrupting. People have a natural tendency to jump in with additional information, correct an error they have noticed, or make a point while it's fresh in their minds. It takes self-discipline to listen attentively, recognizing that your turn will come, especially for "Type A" people who find waiting sheer agony. Or for intolerant people who can't stand to sit quietly while someone rambles on about something they consider to be complete nonsense.

It's true that we cannot learn anything new while we're talking while much can be learned by listening. It's equally true that it's much easier to relate to someone and build interpersonal relationships by listening to what they have to say. But the fact still remains that effective listening is a skill that has to be developed through practice. Slowing down and giving someone your undivided attention consumes time, but it is time well spent.

COMPASSIONATE LISTENING

According to Ethyl Sharp, writing in the *St. Pete's Times* (August 25, 1992), listening is also a way of caring. She writes in the article about working with the elderly and how active listening provides caregivers the means of focusing on the opportunities in relationships and less on the problems.

Psychologists at UCLA asked 55 cancer patients what they considered to be helpful support. The answers did not include practical advice and helpful information from friends and family. The answer was simply good, old-fashioned love, emotional support, and calm concern offered by people who cared about them. The strongest supportive factor was "just being there."

Ethyl Sharp suggests that just sitting quietly and being comfortable with silence opens doors of opportunity to listen to not only words but the emotions underneath.

There is no greater way of displaying kindness and respect than listening attentively to what people have to say. Someone once placed an ad in a mid-western state's newspaper to the effect that they would listen to anyone for twenty minutes without interrupting for five dollars (this was before inflation). They were deluged with phone calls. Listening is the most powerful tool in the communication process. And one that every educator must develop. Stephen Covey sums up the attitude we should have when he says, in his book *The 7 Habits of Highly Effective People*: "Seek first to understand and then to be understood."

BE AN ACTIVE LISTENER

Active listening will help avoid conflict and improve communications. Lean forward to demonstrate your interest in the speaker. Establish eye contact. Resist the temptation to glance at your watch or the door. Devote full attention to the speaker. Don't make judgmental or negative statements. But avoid complete silence as well. The lack of any response suggests you aren't listening. Ask for clarification. Summarize key points and ask if you've interpreted them correctly. Listen for ideas, not details. But hear the person out. Most people are flattered when you listen to them. They respond positively, respect you more. And *your* ideas then tend to have greater influence.

We tend to be too quick to speak, often evaluating or judging others' ideas. Communication cannot take place unless we listen effectively. Often we find ourselves arguing over minor points when in reality we are close to being in agreement, simply because we haven't listened to each other.

Always dwell on what the other person says before responding. Active listening involves paraphrasing what you think the other person said. This gives the person an opportunity to clarify it or modify it or confirm that your interpretation of what was said is entirely accurate. Be sure to empathize with others. Put yourself in their shoes and try to understand why they believe what they do. If you cannot for the life of you understand why they would ever think the way they do, at least admit that they have a right to think that way. Hearing them out may lead to understanding, but bursting in with your own beliefs, with no attempt to see things from their point of view, is inviting conflict.

HANDLING CONFLICT

It is the leadership of the administrator that determines the direction of the school, and it is imperative that you develop a comfortable expertise in handling conflict. Otherwise, antagonism and frayed relationships will cripple effective school undertakings. If you want to change a person's point of view, direct confrontation rarely works. For every action there's an equal and opposite reaction, and trying to force your opinion on someone else will simply cause him/her to resist all the more. When met with resistance, most people push harder. They augment their arguments with facts and figures, examples, and supportive quotes, trying to overwhelm the other person with the rightness of their point of view. Unfortunately, instead of breaking down the other's resistance, it only serves to strengthen it.

You cannot change another person; the person has to change himself. But you can help the person change by being on his side instead of in opposition. This does not mean you have to agree with the person's idea or opinion or plan if you feel it's wrong. But you should be able to agree with something the person said. Find a common meeting ground and start the discussion with a point you both agree on. In this way you are seen as a friend, not a foe. And by being willing to change yourself a little, you are encouraging the other person to change a little in return.

Jerry Richardson and Noel Marculis, in their book *The Magic of Rapport: The Business of Negotiation* (Avon, 1984), refer to this as "pacing." You are pacing someone when you are in agreement or alignment with him. It is a way of establishing rapport with another person. People like people who agree with them and are friendly toward them. And when people like you they tend to agree with you. Once you are "on their side" and supporting an idea that is common to all of you, you are in a position to suggest other options. You can lead them in a different direction.

For example, if someone in a meeting makes an emotional appeal to change the weight of a final exam and cites disadvantage upon disadvantage (imagined or otherwise) of the present system, don't oppose him/her directly even if you are just as adamant that the policy should remain in force. Open by honestly saying that if you were him you would probably feel the same way (naturally you would if you were he). Reinforce your rapport with him by picking one of the disadvantages cited that you agree with. "You are absolutely right when you say it puts an added burden on the teachers, Sam." Then, after discussing that point for a while, you might ask "Is there any way we could possibly get around these disadvantages without actually scrapping the procedure altogether?" You are not seen as "the enemy" trying to oppose his idea, but as a friend who recognizes the validity of his arguments and is willing to make changes. You may, in fact, end up with the current system still intact, with slight modifications and a bonus of having someone supporting the procedure, who was previously undermining it at every opportunity.

COMMUNICATE

According to a study by Hay Research for Management in Philadelphia (reported in the September 1987 issue of *Success Magazine*), companies find there is a relationship between high performance and communication. A similar relationship exists in schools. It has become apparent that the difference between a good school and a truly outstanding school is the quality of the school's culture. And the basis of good school culture is communication.

Time and again surveys indicate the importance of communication, yet time and again in management seminars, people cite "poor communications" as a major problem. The popularity of the various seminars in the communication field seems to indicate a concern as well. But these seminars concentrate on the skills of communication. We learn how to write effectively, conduct meetings more productively, interpret body language accurately, *ad infinitum*. But is there any guarantee we will put any of these skills into practice?

The problem would not appear to be the lack of ability to communicate, but simply the lack of communication. Whether it's due to time limitations, insecurity, forgetfulness, misjudgment, or just plain laziness, there seems to be a problem in taking the time to communicate information to others.

Schools are in the communication business more than ever before. Difficult budget battles require that taxpayers and parents are up to date on the school's programs. A good administrator wants to keep parents informed (and supportive).

Open up the lines of communication. Don't be stingy with the information. Some educators err on the side of giving too little information since they don't want to provide any more information than the person actually needs to perform his or her job. But there is a motivational value to "being in" on things. Teamwork is only developed where information is shared freely. Tell people the *reason* for a policy change, not just the change. We should concentrate less time on developing skills and more time on putting what skills we have into practice.

Although it's great to issue a weekly calendar and monthly newsletter, it cannot replace walking through the building, mingling in the cafeteria, feeling what the teachers feel, talking to staff members. There is a time for "quiet hours" and a time for the personal touch. Both are times well spent.

Don't fall into the trap of spending all your communicating time with the same people. Most people are familiar with Pareto's Principle (or the 80-20 Rule) in reference to time management. We're bombarded with its applications: 80% of the value is derived from 20% of the activities; 80% of the information needed for decision-making is evident during the first 20% of discussion time; 80% of the time spent on the telephone is with 20% of the callers; 80% of the meeting time is spent on the first 20% of the agenda items; *ad infinitum.*

But the 80-20 Rule is just as applicable to communications. Eighty percent of an administrator's time is probably spent with 20% of the teachers (not that they *need* the time, but they're probably either pleasant to be with or chronic gripers). Eighty percent of a principal's comments are made on the 20% of a teacher's job that is performed inadequately. (While the 80% that is performed satisfactorily is virtually ignored). And 80% of the work is performed by 20% of the people.

Look for the 80-20 Rule in *your* relationships. If positive reinforcement does work, why not spend more time commenting on those jobs that are done correctly. Spend time with the people who need help. And balance workloads so the willing person does not continually get the dirty end of the stick. Above all, communicate!

Chapter 11

Make Meetings More Productive

PLAN TO SUCCEED

In a school environment it is not always possible to hold formal meetings. In fact, it is preferable in many cases to meet one-on-one with teachers and staff members where time is of the essence in achieving agreement on a course of action. But whether formal or informal, planning is essential. There should be an objective and an agenda for every meeting. If a 10-minute emergency meeting is necessary, you may have at least a minute to prepare for it. A few scribbled notes on a scratch pad to guide you to the objective are better than winging it.

For more formal meetings, where you have more time to prepare, you might even develop a pre-meeting checklist, as shown in Exhibit 10, so you don't overlook anything during the planning stage. Meetings have a reputation for being time wasters—interruptions to "real work." This should not be the case if you plan well, act on your plan, and evaluate the results.

If an objective can be best attained through a formal meeting, choose the participants carefully. Keep the number of people at the meeting as small as possible. If you invite 10 people, they should accomplish 10 times as much as one person working

Pre-Meeting Checklist

☐ Establish objectives for meeting

☐ Choice of meeting date and time

☐ Selection of meeting/site physical layout

☐ Physical facilities/layout/visual aids

☐ Preparation and mailing of agenda

☐ Advance mailing of reports

☐ Meeting supplies reference materials/props

☐ Formation of meeting files

☐ Accommodations and transportation for out-of-town attendees

☐ Reminder mailing/telephone calls

☐ Coat room/reception area/registration

☐ Assignment of minutes-taking

EXHIBIT 10
Pre-Meeting Checklist

alone at the same problem. The more attendees you invite to a meeting, the longer the meeting lasts. Often people like to make their presence known and will participate in the discussions whether they have anything significant to contribute or not. The more people there are, the more interaction takes place.

Invite only those people who can help reach the meeting's objective(s). They are to be the decision-makers (assuming decisions are to be made)—those whose input is essential to the decision-making process, and those who require information *from* the meeting that cannot be gained as effectively afterwards.

An agenda sent out well in advance of the meeting affords the participants a chance to prepare adequately before the meeting. Make sure you get in the habit of following the agenda as issued. If the meeting never starts as scheduled and never conforms to the agenda, people will start ignoring the agenda when it is received, and adequate preparation will *not* take place. To encourage attendees to think about a problem *before* the meeting starts, try putting the agenda items in the form of questions. For example, instead of simply listing a topic as "Student Attire," record it as "Should students be permitted to wear hats in class?" This allows people to think about it in advance, dig up relevant information, and save unnecessary preamble and discussion time at the meeting.

Exhibit 11 shows a form that could be used for an advance agenda. Exhibit 12 provides an example of how the completed agenda might look. Detail the starting time, ending time, time allocated to each topic area, and the names of those individuals who are responsible for reporting on the various agenda items. Make sure the items are listed in order of importance; if the meeting comes to an abrupt end for some reason, you will at least have addressed the important issues. Items not covered and held over to a future meeting will be those of lesser importance. Poll the participants in advance. Make sure you know what they want discussed and what they have to report. And tell them what you *expect of them*. They should be prepared and aware of the time allocated for their presentation or report. Above all, they should understand the objectives of the meeting. Don't cram too much into the agenda. Skipping quickly over critical issues in order to finish on time is *not* a time saver.

A time saver for meeting participants would be an accurate, clearly marked, map of how to get to the meeting site. If all the meetings are held at one site, so much the better; simply run off a hundred copies of the same map for future use. Don't take it for granted people will remember how to get there. Perhaps someone else drove the last time. Or perhaps he or she didn't

AGENDA

Name of group: _____

Objective: _____

Date: _____ Meeting no.: _____

Starting time: _____ Place: _____

Ending time: _____ Called by: _____

IN ATTENDANCE

IF UNAVAILABLE, RESPOND BY:

TIME	AGENDA ITEM	PERSON RESPONSIBLE	TIME ALLOCATED

EXHIBIT 11
Agenda Form

AGENDA

Name of group: _____ Union Administrative Committee _____

Objective: _____ To update members on relevant issues _____

Date: May 18/93 _____ Meeting no.: ___3_____

Starting time: _____ 3:15 p.m. _____ Place: ___District Office_____

Ending time: _____ 4:30 p.m. _____ Called by: __Robert Orms_____

IN ATTENDANCE

John Matthews	Robert Orms
Bill Jackson	Janet Wakely
Martha Malone	Marlene Wilson
Joe Banks	Colin Wainwright
Jim O'Malley	Stella Murphy

IF UNAVAILABLE, RESPOND BY: May 14/93

TIME	AGENDA ITEM	PERSON RESPONSIBLE	TIME ALLOCATED
3:15 p.m.	Professional Development Report	Bill Jackson	10 min.
3:25 p.m.	Report on survey results of Staff Development Conference	Stella Murphy	20 min.
3:45 p.m.	Strategic plan to implement New Compact for Learning	Robert Orms	35 min.
4:20 p.m.	Explanation of time change at Elementary School	Robert Orms	10 min.
4:30 p.m.	Adjourn		

© Time Management Consultants Inc., 1984

EXHIBIT 12
Sample Agenda

attend the last meeting. If the meeting is held in your school, and people from a different school are invited, the same applies. In fact, it's a good idea to have on hand a map of directions to get to your school anyway; people intending to visit you will appreciate the courtesy.

Ask that any lengthy reports be distributed at least one week before the meeting. If lengthy reports containing recommendations are not circulated well in advance of the meeting, the meeting could be ineffective. Not only is time lost reading the reports during the meeting, but chances are they will only be given a cursory glance. Decisions to accept recommendations could be made without a thorough knowledge of the facts. The person presenting the report is no doubt well prepared, but everyone else is at a disadvantage.

If you want to emphasize the high cost of meetings and motivate attendees to keep meeting-time to a minimum, distribute Exhibit 13 with every agenda you send out. Or distribute it with any handout materials. If you know the approximate average hourly pay out for a particular meeting, circle the figure which corresponds to the cost per minute of that meeting.

You may want to control the seating arrangement as well. If you allow people to sit where they please, you may end up with "buddies" sharing experiences, extroverts sharing stories, or hotheads sharing arguments while the meeting is in progress. Use place cards to predetermine the seating, and separate individuals you feel may come into conflict with one another or share jokes. Seat protagonists on the same side of the table so they won't have eye contact; separate comedians with a quiet, serious type, etc.

Planned seating can help move the meeting along faster, with fewer distractions. Make the name cards big, and print the names legibly. They will assist the person taking the minutes as well as those participants who don't know everyone. Exhibit 14 illustrates a tent card which displays "Guidelines for Participants" to make everyone aware of their responsibilities during the meeting.

Don't make the surroundings too comfortable or the meeting may degenerate into a social event. When the participants are

What is the Cost Per Minute of a Meeting

No of Participants	Average Hourly Wage of Participants						
	$15	$20	$25	$30	$35	$40	$45
2	.50	.67	.83	1.00	1.17	1.33	1.50
3	.75	1.00	1.24	1.50	1.75	2.00	2.25
4	1.00	1.33	1.66	2.00	2.33	2.66	3.00
5	1.25	1.67	2.07	2.50	2.92	3.33	3.75
6	1.50	2.00	2.48	3.00	3.50	3.99	4.50
7	1.75	2.33	2.90	3.50	4.07	4.67	5.25
8	2.00	2.66	3.32	4.00	4.67	5.32	6.00
9	2.25	3.00	3.73	4.50	5.25	6.00	6.75
10	2.50	3.34	4.14	5.00	5.83	6.66	7.50
11	2.75	3.67	4.56	5.50	6.41	7.33	8.25
12	3.00	4.00	4.96	6.00	7.00	8.00	9.00
13	3.25	4.34	5.39	6.50	7.58	8.67	9.75
14	3.50	4.66	5.83	7.00	8.14	9.34	10.50
15	3.75	5.01	6.25	7.50	8.75	10.00	11.25
16	4.00	5.33	6.67	8.00	9.34	10.64	12.00
17	4.25	5.68	7.08	8.50	9.92	11.33	12.75
18	4.50	6.00	7.50	9.00	10.50	12.00	13.50
19	4.75	6.35	7.91	9.50	11.08	12.66	14.25
20	5.00	6.68	8.33	10.00	11.66	13.32	15.00
21	5.25	6.93	8.74	10.50	12.24	14.00	15.75
22	5.50	7.35	9.17	11.00	12.82	14.66	16.50
23	5.75	7.66	9.57	11.50	13.40	15.33	17.25
24	6.00	8.00	10.00	12.00	14.00	16.00	18.00
25	6.25	8.33	10.41	12.50	14.58	16.67	18.75
26	6.50	8.67	10.83	13.00	15.16	17.34	19.50
27	6.75	9.00	11.25	13.50	15.74	18.00	20.25
28	7.00	9.33	11.67	14.00	16.28	18.68	21.00
29	7.25	9.67	12.09	14.50	16.86	19.33	21.75
30	7.50	10.00	12.50	15.00	17.50	20.00	22.50

EXHIBIT 13
Cost/Minute of Meetings

treated to coffee, donuts, ice water, comfortable chairs ,and access to a telephone, you must realize that there will be distractions, side conversations, interruptions, and generally poor attentiveness. You don't send out for coffee and cakes every time you invite someone into your office, so why do it for

GUIDELINES FOR PARTICIPANTS

- SPEAK UP. DON'T SAVE COMMENTS FOR THE WALK OUT THE DOOR.
- DON'T MONOPOLIZE THE TIME. GIVE EVERYONE A CHANCE TO SPEAK.
- RESPECT OTHER PEOPLE'S IDEAS. WHEN DISAGREEING, BE POSITIVE AND CONSTRUCTIVE.
- IF SOMETHING IS UNCLEAR, ASK. IT MAY BE UNCLEAR TO OTHERS AS WELL.
- DON'T CARRY ON SIDE CONVERSATIONS. MAINTAIN AN ACTIVE INTEREST IN THE MEETING.
- ASK YOURSELF "HOW CAN I BE BETTER PREPARED FOR THE NEXT MEETING?"

EXHIBIT 14
Meeting Tent Card

a two-hour meeting involving many people? If you feel obligated to feed their stomachs as well as their minds, promise coffee and donuts *after* the meeting—it may speed things up a bit.

For longer meetings, it's okay to have coffee available before or after a meeting and during one of the scheduled breaks, but why the compulsion to provide continuous coffee service *during* the meeting? It's distracting, discourteous and messy to have people continually refilling their cups and rattling china and silverware while presentations are being made or discussions are in progress. Clear away the coffee, refreshments, and snacks once the meeting is underway (on time) and concentrate on the business at hand. Remember, it's a meeting room, not a cafeteria. When you do schedule a break, stick to the schedule. Before breaking, tell the group both the amounts of time to be taken, and the exact time the meeting will resume.

Develop a meeting-room checklist similar to the one shown in Exhibit 15 to ensure that nothing has been overlooked. Planning prevents problems.

ACT ON YOUR PLAN

Keep the meeting active. Start it on time, no exceptions. If you're the only one there on time, talk to yourself until the others arrive! Don't recap with every late arrival. Delaying the meeting simply encourages lateness. At the start, review the agenda. Restate the objectives. Keep to the agenda and don't allow participants to take off on tangents.

If someone starts a trivial conversation, politely cut him or her off with a remark such as "I know that problem's in good hands with you, Jack. We won't discuss it here." Remember, if your meeting starts to drift in a direction that will not help reach your objective, pull it back on course. The name of the game is to get results. This does not mean you should rush through the agenda items themselves. You must discuss each item thoroughly and allow enough time for input. But spend time in proportion to the importance of the item. You wouldn't

Meeting Room
Checklist

- ☐ Tables and chairs
- ☐ Ashtrays/no-smoking signs
- ☐ Writing materials
- ☐ Handouts/reports/spare agendas/programs
- ☐ Water/glasses/serviettes
- ☐ Name tags/place cards
- ☐ Message board outside rooms
- ☐ Lighting/temperature control/sound system
- ☐ AV equipment/projector/screen/flipchart
- ☐ Extension cord/outlets
- ☐ Lectern/podium/pointer/gavel
- ☐ Microphone(s)
- ☐ Tape recorder/tapes
- ☐ Coffee/juice
- ☐ Room identification and direction signs
- ☐ Coat check arrangements
- ☐ Reception/registration

EXHIBIT 15
Meeting Room Checklist

waste a lot of time discussing the menu for a staff Christmas party, but a decision to change class schedules or expand the counseling services warrants the necessary expenditure of that precious commodity called time. Keep the meeting moving at a brisk pace so people don't become bored and lethargic. Don't allow the meeting to get bogged down in irrelevant discussion. If you do, a meeting that started at 9:00 a.m. sharp may finally end at 9:00 p.m. dull.

Stick to the agenda, and even then, limit the amount of time on each topic. Sure, you may miss a few good ideas, but you'll probably get 80% of the results on a particular topic during the first 20% of the time you've allotted to that topic. Then you must decide whether it is necessary to pursue that topic or problem further. Will any further ideas justify the time spent?

Guard against one or two people monopolizing the discussion, and encourage everyone to participate. Watch for those nonverbal signals that indicate someone doesn't understand, objects, or wishes to speak. Listen more than you talk. One study revealed that the average leader took 60 percent of the conference time. If it's one-way communication you want, forget about a meeting and send a memo instead.

The meeting is over when you have accomplished your objectives, so don't let it drag on. Summarize the action to be taken and make sure responsibilities are clear. A brief summary not only communicates to those present that the meeting is over, it also ensures that they clearly understand their responsibilities as a result of the meeting. Thus a few closing statements, such as "As I understand it, Bill, your committee will address the issue of students wearing hats in class and will send a copy of your recommendations to everyone at this meeting by December 15 . . ." makes for better communication. Don't let the meeting drag out. Conversation prompted by the chairperson's final invitation, "Is there anything else you'd like to discuss before we adjourn?," is usually nonproductive. Don't encourage attendees to drag out the meeting. If a comprehensive agenda was distributed *ahead* of the meeting, there should be no surprises at the *end* of the meeting.

If the meeting is finished and you plan to hold another one, decide the date, time and place right then, while everyone is there. They can block out the required time in their planning calendars immediately. There will be fewer excuses for not being able to make it if they agree to the date and time well in advance. But never call another meeting simply to follow up on assignments already made. Ask for memos, reports or telephone calls instead.

EVALUATE THE ACTION

Always evaluate your formal meetings afterwards. Ask what could be improved next time. Did you start and end on time? Were the objectives reached? Did any of the agenda times drag out? Was everyone's presence necessary? Did all attendees participate? You might distribute an evaluation form similar to the one shown in Exhibit 16.

If you are chairing meetings that are called on a regular basis with the same attendees present each time (committee, task force, departmental meeting, etc.) it is important to let the group have a say in what should be evaluated. Few people appreciate something that is being forced upon them. It is difficult for someone to achieve goals he has no part in forming. Exhibit 16 could be used as a starting point, with additions and changes being made as the group reviews the objectives of the committee.

The group could also agree to draw up self-evaluation forms to be used as a checklist after the meeting or as a guide during the meeting. It could contain questions such as: Did I fulfill my role as a member of this group? Did I participate to the best of my ability? Were there times when I hogged the discussion? Did I press my point too hard? Did I back down too easily? Did I respect the other person's right to voice an opinion? Did I display any outbursts of anger, sarcasm or criticism?

Regardless of the specific questions agreed upon by the group, the last question on a self-evaluation form should ask what could be done differently the next time. The purpose of a self-evaluation form is to (a) get the participants to agree as to what is considered to be proper behavior at meetings, (b) have

Meeting Evaluation Form

Please rate the effectiveness of our meeting by circling the appropriate number ("1" is poor and "5" is excellent).

AREA	RATING	COMMENTS
Did we accomplish our objective?	1 2 3 4 5	
Did we manage our time well?	1 2 3 4 5	
Did everyone have the opportunity to participate?	1 2 3 4 5	
Did any item take too long?	1 2 3 4 5	
Did we stick to the agenda?	1 2 3 4 5	
Were the right people present?	1 2 3 4 5	
Had advance preparation taken place?	1 2 3 4 5	
Were the meeting facilities appropriate	1 2 3 4 5	
Did we end on time?	1 2 3 4 5	

What can I recommend in order to improve the next meeting of this group?

_____

_____

_____

_____

_____

_____

_____

_____

_____

EXHIBIT 16
Meeting Evaluation Form

the participants recognize any unsatisfactory behavior in themselves, and (c) make changes in that behavior so as to improve the quality of their participation and thereby increase the effectiveness of the meeting.

It seems strange that most volunteer organizations ask for the resignation of those committee members who miss a lot of meetings, yet retain those who attend all the meetings and contribute nothing. If you want to be time effective, the attendees must be both active *and* productive.

As chairperson, you may also wish to draw up an evaluation form or checklist to ensure that you have a good reading on the workings of the group. You might ask yourself such questions as: What were the meeting's goals, and did we achieve them? Who were the most helpful participants? What special abilities and talents were revealed by the participants? What problems arose during the meeting? Did someone speak too much, or too little? Did I successfully draw out quiet members of the group? Did I allow everyone to participate? Were there any bad feelings as a result of decisions made? What can I do differently next time to improve the meeting?

Evaluation of meetings is important for both continued improvement in the caliber of meetings held and for continued growth and development of the participants. But it must be positive and nonjudgmental. At no time should the meeting's participants feel they are being graded on their performance. The evaluation form should be seen as a group effort to provide guidance and direction and to help improve the effectiveness of the meetings.

If your magic-markers ran dry or the overhead transparency bulb burned out and you had no spare, it should never happen a second time. *Planning for any meeting starts with the end of the last meeting*. Inadequate planning steals precious time. If you want to check the cost of this time, take another look at Exhibit 13. If you have 10 people in attendance, earning an average of $20 per hour, the meeting is costing you $3.34 *per minute*. If you only lose 15 minutes looking for a spare bulb or magic-marker, this simple slip in planning has cost you $50.10. With the same table, you can see that a four-hour meeting will cost you $801.60. And that's an understatement because time spent in meetings is time taken away from other critical activities. Judge the importance of a meeting by the results you get from it. *Because it's costing you!*

When you issue the minutes, prepare a cover page using the

form shown in Exhibit 17. It highlights the decisions reached, the action required, the person responsible for initiating the action, and the date any action is to be completed. People frequently fail to read through their minutes properly and as a result fail to take prompt action following the meeting. This one-page summary strips them of any excuse for overlooking their responsibilities.

In meetings where it's not essential that discussions or motions be recorded, the form can actually *replace* the minutes. What a timesaver that will be! It's important that people start on their assignments as soon as possible after the meeting. So encourage them to make their own notes. Issue "Meeting Participant's Action Sheets" (described later) or give them a copy of your own notes immediately after the meeting. Don't let them wait for the minutes to be typed and issued before they initiate any action.

ADVICE FOR ATTENDEES

You may be invited to a meeting as a participant, not a chairperson. Attending meetings when your presence is un- necessary is a costly error. So the minute you receive a meeting notice, contact the chairperson to determine whether your presence is essential. You may have been invited as a matter of protocol or habit. Perhaps receiving a copy of the minutes will suffice. If it's important that you receive information (which is only available through attendance), consider sending someone else. If you must attend in person, determine whether you can attend only a portion of the meeting. But if the necessity of your personal attendance at the entire meeting is confirmed, waste no time in getting organized and doing your part to make the meeting as effective as possible.

Make notes as the meeting progresses. Use the "Meeting Participant's Action Sheet" (Exhibit 18) to summarize the decisions reached, action required, whose responsibility it is to initiate the action, and the date that action is to be completed. With this summary sheet you won't have to wait for the

Meeting Action Sheet

TIME INSTITUTE

Name of group: _____

Objectives: _____

Agenda	In Attendance

Decisions Reached

Action Required	Responsibility	Completion Date

EXHIBIT 17
Meeting Action Sheet

MEETING PARTICIPANTS ACTION SHEET

NAME OF GROUP: _____ DATE: _____

IN ATTENDANCE: _____

AGENDA ITEM	DECISION REACHED	ACTION REQUIRED	PERSON RESPONSIBLE	COMPLETION DATE

© 1988 Harold Taylor Time Consultants Inc.

EXHIBIT 18

Meeting Participant's Action Sheet

minutes to arrive before you take action. You will also be able to spot any errors in the minutes. And if there *are* no minutes, these notes are a *must*.

The "Meeting Participant's Action Sheet" will also enable you to keep the meeting on track even though you are not the chairperson. If you find the group discussing an agenda item before a decision was reached on a previous item, you can break in with "Excuse me, Jack, I didn't hear the decision reached on the previous item." Groups frequently drift to other items inadvertently, and you can quickly bring this to their attention.

Don't be a passive attendee. Help move the meeting along. If you see that it's approaching the lunch hour and there's only about an hour of business left to be conducted, suggest that lunch be delayed until the meeting is finished. Don't let time be wasted on another meeting "start-up" unless absolutely necessary. If someone starts discussing something that's not on the agenda, bring it to the chairperson's attention immediately. If someone starts a side conversation with you, politely say, "Excuse me" and direct your remarks or attention to the business at hand. Maintain interest in the meeting, not in your surroundings.

If the meeting is boring, you may have to help liven it up by raising your own level of interest. Be cheerful, enthusiastic and positive. You're not the only one in the room who's bored, so your fellow participants will appreciate your efforts.

If the meeting is finished, and you know there is going to be another one, try to get a date, time and place decided right then, while everyone is still together. Then you can schedule it in your planning diary and commence your preparation immediately. There will be fewer excuses for not being able to make the next meeting if everyone agrees on a date well in advance.

Chapter 12

Coping With Stress

CONTROL YOUR REACTION

Let's face it, we're living in a stressful world and there's little we can do to change it. Today's administrator, whether a superintendent, principal or chairperson, is more accountable today than ever before. Intelligent parents and overtaxed residents are demanding more and more. The government is mandating more each year. Content taught in college 30 years ago is in the seventh grade curriculum now. People in education are running faster than ever before. Environmental stress takes its toll in terms of physical and psychological problems. But even though we can usually do little to control our environment, we can do much to control our reaction to it. Therein lies the secret of coping with stress.

Stress is best described as the "fight or flight response"—an involuntary body response which increases our blood pressure, heart rate, breathing rate, blood flow to the muscles and metabolism—preparing us to face some conflict or flee some danger. The body is prepared for some physical activity, but the activity never comes because most of today's situations, particularly in an educational environment, call for behavioral

153

adjustments, not physical activity. Consequently, our body's systems are thrown out of balance.

The fight or flight response could be elicited when you are suddenly cut off by another car during your hectic drive to the school one morning. The body's responses prepare you for "flight" but instead you sit there and stew—your hands clenching the wheel, face flushed, stomach muscles tight. The appropriate response might be to jump out of the car, yank open the antagonist's door, pull him out by the scruff of the neck and smack him a good one. Although this would invariably relieve the tension, it is only appropriate from the viewpoint of our body's system and not from the viewpoint of socially acceptable behavior. Consequently, we remain under stress long after the cause of it has disappeared.

The thoughtless motorist does not put us under stress, nor does the irate superintendent, the careless teacher, the stubborn student or the misplaced file. It is our *reactions* to these daily incidents that cause the grief. Instead of saying "His attitude upset me," we would be more accurate in saying "I upset myself by my reaction to his attitude."

You can seldom control what other people say, but you can control yourself and how you *react* to what other people say. It's not easy. The first step is to admit that you are, in fact, upsetting yourself. Talk yourself into relaxing. Say to yourself, "Hey fellow, calm down. You're starting to upset yourself again." Getting upset—putting yourself under stress—will not help solve the problem. Convince yourself of that fact. Reason with yourself. In time, you will find it actually works. But it requires a commitment on your part to take control of your own life and not to let yourself be controlled by others.

DON'T LET HASSLES GET YOU DOWN

Richard Lazarus, writing in the July 1981 issue of *Psychology Today*, reported that minor daily events such as losing a wallet or getting caught in a traffic jam can be more harmful than infrequent, major events such as divorce, retirement or being fired.

Those minor daily events have a great effect on our needs and our health. These effects vary according to their frequency, intensity and our reactions to them. When under pressure, those petty problems can have a much greater effect than if they had occurred at less anxious times. Stress is not caused by the event itself, but by our reaction to it.

Among the top hassles revealed in a survey were: Misplacing or losing things and too many things to do. Time management will certainly help out with these two. Organizing yourself and your environment should alleviate the first problem, and getting rid of the trivia in your life and concentrating on priorities should relieve the other hassle.

Regardless of how effectively we manage our time, there will always be some hassle in our lives. Lazarus suggests that uplifts may serve as emotional buffers against disorders brought on by hassles. Uplifts include such activities as enjoying yourself with good friends, spending time with the family, eating out, and getting enough sleep.

And don't forget the importance of your reaction to hassles. If you can shrug them off or even laugh at them without letting them get you all tense and upset, you've got them licked.

Check those hassles which you have experienced during the past week. It could be you are deluged with "minor" annoyances that precipitate feelings of stress. Remember, it's your reactions to these incidents that can cause the damage:

* You misplaced or lost something.
* You spent at least 15 minutes searching for things.
* You have been concerned about your physical appearance.
* You have had too many things to do.
* You have been concerned about your weight.
* You were upset about the way in which a staff member performed his/her job.
* You have a disagreement with someone at school.
* You were stuck in a traffic jam on the way to or from school.

- You were involved in or present during an accident in the building or schoolyard.

- You were dissatisfied with the quality of a job you performed.

- You didn't have time for breakfast one morning.

- You have to prod others to get on with what they were trying to say.

- You became annoyed at having to wait for someone.

- You had to stand in line at the copier, cafeteria, or to see someone.

- You were put on "hold" while telephoning someone.

- You were interrupted in the middle of an important job by the superintendent, a staff member, or a teacher several times in the same day.

- You frequently had to respond to the telephone at inconvenient times.

- You were anxious to get rid of a salesperson who persisted in dragging out the conversation.

- You had to attend a meeting when you could not afford the time.

- You were held up on a task with which you were anxious to proceed because of slow decision-making or response on the part of someone else.

- You were given a rush job to do with an unrealistic deadline.

- You had to juggle priorities more than twice due to more pressing jobs cropping up.

- You forgot something, which caused embarrassment as well as inconvenience.

- You said "yes" to something which you later regretted.

- You had to perform an unpleasant task.

If you have checked off 10 or more of these hassles, you could be susceptible to stress-related disorders, such as insomnia, ulcers or even heart attack. But remember, it's your *reaction* to these hassles that causes the damage, so don't take them too seriously. Put them in their proper perspective. For instance, what effect is being stuck in a traffic jam and being late for work going to have on your profession, your future, and your life? Also, be sure to pamper yourself with enough of those "uplifts" that Lazarus has recommended.

MANAGING YOUR HEALTH

There's more to management than MBO and Zero Base Budgeting. The mind cannot function without a body and the body takes its share of lumps as a result of the stressful conditions under which educators must operate. We can avoid some stress and alleviate some stress, but there is no way we are going to eliminate it completely. Nor do we want to—because a little stress keeps us at our fighting best. But we can never tell when "a little" becomes "too much" and one of the few defenses we have against the ravages of too much stress is a healthy body. The most valuable resource of any administrator is his or her health, yet many of us spend more effort and money in managing our time or developing our skills.

In this age of automobiles, elevators and laborsaving gadgetry, our normal work activities do not provide the exercise which our bodies—muscles, hearts, and lungs—require if they are to continue to function efficiently and effectively. An aerobic exercise program, such as the one advocated by Dr. Kenneth H. Cooper, will develop cardiovascular fitness and allow us to more effectively withstand the stresses of modern living. The body that isn't used deteriorates. The lungs become inefficient, the heart grows weaker, the blood vessels less pliable and we become more vulnerable to illness. Our mental state is also affected by inactivity. We become lethargic, depressed and easily fatigued.

The best exercises are believed to be those that place sufficient demand on the lungs, heart and blood system to produce the training effect. Included in this category are running, swimming, cycling, walking, stationary running, handball, basketball, and squash.

If you have been inactive for a long time, it is unwise to plunge headlong into a strenuous exercise program. Many fitness institutes have excellent programs which require a thorough medical checkup prior to their commencement.

One of the safest, simplest, most effective, albeit most underrated, exercise is just plain walking. One executive health report claims that walking is a significant modifier of the natural aging process. It is important to the circulation of the blood, helps protect you from the complications of arteriosclerosis, aids in the treatment of diabetes, may help induce sleep, and is beneficial in counteracting stress. The distance you go is far more important than the speed at which you travel, and the report claims that if you run hard for six miles, you burn up only 20% more calories than you do walking the same distance.

There is more to health than exercise, of course, and we must examine the hazards of obesity, smoking, high blood pressure, excessive alcohol, and various physical and mental ailments. Regular checkups followed by corrective action if necessary and dedication to a healthful lifestyle are prerequisites of an effective administrator.

There is as much, if not more, written on health than on education. Perhaps, because of this, we tend to ignore most of it and devote our valuable time to researching the literature of our chosen field. But we should reexamine our priorities. Assembling the facts, determining your present condition, planning a strategy for improvement and implementing that strategy in order to achieve your predetermined goal is an outline for the most critical, vital and effective management technique of all time—the technique of *managing your health.*

AVOIDING BURNOUT

Keep your job—and your life—in perspective. With so much emphasis on success and achievement it sometimes becomes difficult to relax and enjoy life. Don't set your sights too high. Do the best you can, but don't kill yourself. Job burnout is a result of too much stress, and most jobs are stressful enough without adding your own unrealistic goals and expectations.

Set realistic goals. And realize that you can't do everything. Work on priorities—the 20% of the activities which will bring you 80% of the results.

And always have some way of working off mental and emotional stress. Engage in a regular exercise program. Have interests other than your job. Make it a habit to talk over your problems with a close friend. Above all, remember that what you *are* is more important than what you *do*.

It's possible that you work harder and faster under the pressure of unrealistic deadlines, but it's doubtful that you work **better**. Excellence does not come from tired, harried people. Mediocrity does. You would hate to have your plane piloted by someone who had been flying steadily for 12 hours. And you probably wouldn't feel too comfortable in a taxi if the driver had been driving all night. It's a fact that tired workers cause accidents. For the same reason, most skiing mishaps take place during that "one last run."

Don't talk yourself into believing that working steadily with your nose to the grindstone will lead to success. It will only lead to a flat nose. Work smarter, not harder. Concentrate on the goals you set for yourself. Every day do something to bring yourself closer to them. But recognize that you will have to ignore some of those unimportant activities that produce minimal results. You can't do everything and still keep your life in balance.

Vacations should be blocked off in your calendar ahead of anything else. Relaxation is necessary in order to keep your mind alert, your body healthy, and your family together. As one educator claims, "Pausing to attend a funeral is not a time waster unless it's your own."

Some people take better care of their office equipment than they do their own bodies. The human body is a lot more valuable than machinery. And with a little care it may have a longer life. But one thing it doesn't have is a warranty or money-back guarantee. There are no returns or allowances. So spend all the time and money necessary for preventative maintenance.

To prevent yourself from filling your planning calendar with only work-related activities, schedule blocks of leisure time. Those outings with the children, that movie with your spouse, that tennis game or shopping trip. Schedule them in ink, not pencil; make them definite, not tentative. Most people schedule them with the idea that they will go through with it "if something more important doesn't come up." And the "something more important" is usually job-related, and usually involves value in terms of dollars and cents.

Recognize that leisure time has value too. Not in terms of measurable "dollars and cents," but in terms of long-term effectiveness; in terms of family accord and happiness; in terms of physical health and mental alertness.

THE POWER OF LAUGHTER

According to an article in the *Toronto Star* (March 23, 1987), humor can boost your health and wealth. Reporting on a conference on the power of laughter and play, the article quoted 82-year-old anthropologist Ashley Montagu: "Adults are nothing more than deteriorated children." When people laugh hard the heart rate speeds up, the circulatory system is stimulated, and muscles go limp.

Barbara Mackoff, author of *Leaving the Office Behind* (Dell, 1984), believes humor can help us relieve stress produced by work. And Norman Cousins, in his book *Anatomy of An Illness* (Bantam, 1981), gives an amazing account of the therapeutic value of laughter as he relates his own successful fight against a crippling disease. He also describes other work that has been conducted on the beneficial aspects of laughter. Although the research is not plentiful, it indicates that laughter and attitude contribute to a healthy lifestyle and possibly "cure" illness. Sigmund Freud, for one, believed that mirth was a highly useful way of counteracting nervous tension, and that humor could be used as effective therapy.

As Cousins points out, the effect of uncontrollable laughter is relaxation "almost to the point of an open sprawl." It is as tangible as any other form of physical exercise.

Although *Candid Camera*, Marx Brothers films, and books on humor were part of his self-prescribed medicine, there is another necessary ingredient. It is summed up in this statement by Norman Cousins: "I learned that a highly developed purpose and the will to live are among the prime raw materials of human existence."

An article in the *Toronto Star* by Paul Watson was headed, "Laughter—The Key to the First 100 Years." The article described a Oakville, Ontario, resident, Rita Hubbard, who was celebrating her 100th birthday. At the time, she was still adding to her more than 2,000 hours of volunteer work and reading at least three books a week. Her secret? "I'm just an ordinary old woman, but I've spent my whole life laughing. I believe in looking on the bright side of things."

Laughter enables us to cope with the myriad of hassles we encounter every day—from irate parents to disruptive students. According to Zindel Segal, a psychologist at Toronto Clarke Institute of Psychiatry, these minor annoyances can be harmful because they have a way of accumulating. All these little annoyances mount up; people are continually more frustrated and irritated. If they have no way of releasing the anger, they can become chronically upset or chronically unhappy, and could take it out on other people.

The solution? Segal suggests we try to find the humor in a situation. And put it in its right perspective. Realize you can't do anything about it, and relax.

I don't know whether there are statistics that prove that cheerful people live longer, but there's enough evidence to suggest that laughter at least improves the quality of life. So let's not take life, and ourselves, too seriously. Be quick to listen, slow to anger, and ready to laugh!

Chapter 13

Manage Yourself

DIVE INTO THE DAY

Some people go swimming an inch at a time. They stick a toe into the water and, shocked by the temperature, commence to first immerse a foot, then two legs, followed by a torso. It's an agonizing process. Each step into deeper water brings another cold shock to the warm body. Eventually they are totally immersed, and pleasantly surprised at how comfortable the water really is.

Many of us approach the day the same way. We get up slowly, dawdle over a second cup of coffee, arrange our materials, procrastinate by first watering the plants, sharpening pencils, rearranging books, straightening our desk. An inch at a time, we ease ourselves into the day, only to discover that the jobs we dreaded were not that bad after all.

How much faster and easier if we would dive into the day as we would dive into a swimming pool, cutting out most of the preliminaries and getting on with the job at hand.

Surgeons take advantage of peak energy levels during early morning hours and schedule operations accordingly. If you are an "early person," don't waste one minute of this valuable period of the day. Do your priority jobs first, and leave the morning newspaper, coffee ritual and desk straightening until later.

One recent seminar attendee told me that he had to get up at 6:00 a.m. in order to drive the distance to my time management seminar:

> "What are you getting up at this hour for?," his wife had asked.

> "To drive to Toronto. I'm attending a seminar on time management," he had explained.

> "Well, if you got up this early every morning, you wouldn't *have* to go to a time management seminar," she had responded.

She was partly right. Early risers get a head start on life. They have the *opportunity* to get more accomplished during that relatively quiet time than they would if they arose in the midst of humanity's "rush hour." If you dawdle in the mornings and roll over for an extra 10 minutes shuteye, try changing your habits.

If you have more energy in the mornings, reserve that time for your priority tasks, whether they are classroom evaluations, goal setting, or budget preparation. You may not be able to see many people early in the morning, but at least schedule those high priority tasks that relate to your main work objectives for that day. Even if the rest of the day is fragmented by interruptions, telephone calls, meetings and rush jobs, you will at least have accomplished the important high-payoff tasks. And you are more likely to do a good job if you are indeed an "early person."

Never leave important items until later in the day simply because you feel there may be more time later. Time always seems to dissipate faster as the day goes on. It's better to start a job and not complete it that day than never to start it at all.

The same thing applies to your personal life. Most people agree that exercise is more important than making beds, but we all know which activity gets the priority treatment.

Build up some early morning momentum and you'll be able to coast through the day with less difficulty. Physics tells us that an object in motion tends to stay in motion and an object at rest tends to stay at rest. The same law applies to human endeavor. Overcome your daily inertia with a burst of early morning enthusiasm. Once you get rolling, you can plow through those daily tasks and achieve your daily objectives.

But above all, make sure you *have* daily objectives. Don't look at today as an extension of yesterday. Look upon it as an independent unit of time. Set daily goals that tie into your weekly, monthly and annual goals. Judge your performance on a daily basis. Before you retire each night determine whether you accomplished what you set out to do that morning.

DON'T PROCRASTINATE

Why do we put things off? We realize that the present is all we have — that tomorrow may be too late. We are also aware that putting off today's tasks simply adds to tomorrow's burdens. And none of us wants to be one of those people who spends their whole lives preparing to live and never getting around to enjoying each moment as it comes. And yet we procrastinate. Why?

Well, first we have to understand what procrastination really is. Some things have to be delayed; others should be delayed. But if we put off doing high priority activities by doing low priority activities instead, we are procrastinating. We straighten our desk, sharpen our pencils, empty the wastebasket, instead of writing a position paper on gang violence in the schools. We sweep the sidewalk, putter in the garden, smooth the kinks out of the garden hose instead of taking the kids on an excursion to Wonderland. We thumb through magazines, read the paper, watch TV, instead of getting started on that article we've always wanted to write.

Priorities differ from person to person. A kinkless garden hose may be more important to someone than exercise or recreation or family time. But we all know what our own priorities are. They are those meaningful activities which, when completed, bring a sense of achievement and satisfaction. They are the activities which help to attain those personal and professional goals and desires which burn within us.

It is amazing how adept we are at thinking of other things to do when facing an important task. You would think that we would be enthusiastic about an activity that would produce gain, satisfaction, achievement. Unfortunately the satisfaction is not always immediate. The gain is not always something we can readily perceive. Few things worthwhile come without effort, inconvenience, or discomfort. Our natural tendency is to avoid unpleasantness. So we sacrifice long-term benefits in favor of those minor, short-term rewards.

It's only natural to want to relax after dinner instead of washing dishes, even though the delayed task will be even more difficult after the food stains have been allowed to harden. And who could fault us for leaving the broken stair unrepaired until after the football game, even though it presents a safety hazard? And sleeping in on Sunday morning requires less effort than taking the family to church. There is always a diversion at hand to make shirking our responsibility to others and ourselves more palatable.

Sometimes procrastination has minor consequences. At other times, it results in death, injury, or unfulfilled lives. There is even the odd time that procrastination produces *favorable* results (and oh, how we love to rationalize our habit by recalling those occasions). But the habit of procrastination, regardless of the results, is self-defeating in the long run. It makes us feel guilty because we realize it's wrong. It's debilitating because we're constantly dreading the task being postponed. We're more tired mentally by not doing something than we would be physically if we were to do it.

The activity we are postponing could be unpleasant in itself, such as weeding the garden —if that's an activity that we deem unpleasant. Or its magnitude could be unpleasant. An activity such as writing a book could be overwhelming if we dwell on the length of time it would take. We tend to put off tasks that are either unpleasant for us—such as writing statistical reports, doing the laundry, or reprimanding a staff member—or those that will take an overwhelming length of time—such as saving

$5,000 for a trip to Europe, finishing a rec room or writing a book.

To overcome the habit of procrastination, we must generate some enthusiasm to offset the unpleasantness. We must concentrate, not on the activity, but on the reward awaiting us upon completion. If the activity is unpleasant, let us pounce on it immediately and complete it so we won't have to dwell on its unpleasantness. If it's an overwhelming activity, let us chop it up into manageable chunks and polish it off a piece at a time. If we have to drive to the other coast, let's aim at driving six hours each day. If we have to write a book, let's aim at completing ten typewritten pages each day. If we have to pack the contents of a house in preparation for moving, let's aim at packing two cartons each day.

Author Ari Kiev once wrote "When you postpone your involvement in something, you will probably never accomplish it, and will be left with memories of past wishes rather than past deeds." Yesterday will never come again, and tomorrow may never arrive; but today is ours. Let's make the most of it.

SAY "NO" MORE OFTEN

It's so *easy* to say "yes." In fact, you receive immediate rewards—a sense of satisfaction, a feeling of self-worth, praise and gratitude from the other person, but it's short-lived. It's replaced by a feeling of panic, pressure, a sense of hopelessness that you have taken on more than you can possibly handle.

Why don't we say "no" more often? Part of the reason is that we want to be liked. Respected. Admired. It's great for our feeling of self-worth. It's a great feeling to be able to do things for other people. It's great to be needed! But look at the price we have to pay. Stress. Worry. A sense of time urgency. And frequently illness—precipitated by excessive demands on our time.

It takes self-discipline to say "no." But it's worth it. So force yourself to say "no" for a while. It becomes easier, the more you say it. Don't worry about not being liked. What do *you* think of someone who agrees to everything and then never delivers? It's better to decline now than to let somebody down later.

Don't provide a long "excuse" when you say "no." If you qualify a negative reply with a statement such as "I really don't think I'm qualified, or I'd do it," they'll convince you that you are qualified. Or if you say you don't have time, they'll tell you how **little** time it really takes. Simply say "No, I can't. But I appreciate you asking me," and leave it at that. You don't owe anybody a long drawn-out explanation.

Many of us find it difficult to say "no" when turned to for help because we feel our reasons for *not* agreeing to take on the task might not be convincing enough. We don't want people to resent us or lose respect for us. And saying "no" seems so distasteful that it's easier to do the job than risk alienation. It's more *comfortable* at the time to say "yes."

But the same is true for a lot of things. Think how painful it was the first time you had to stand up in front of a class to present a lesson, introduce yourself to a stranger at a party or speak up at a meeting. And yet most of us have overcome our fear of such situations. And we can overcome our fear of saying "no" in the same way—by forcing ourselves to do it again and again until our fear dissipates to a feeling of discomfort. It will never be enjoyable, or shouldn't be, because we are disappointing someone; but it will be tolerable and not upsetting. By saying "no" more often to the activities which we shouldn't be involved in, we are able to spend more time on those meaningful activities which will help us reach our goals.

If someone asks you to serve on a committee, and you cannot afford the time nor can you see any benefit from it, don't hesitate. Don't give the impression you are considering it. Say "no" immediately. Provide a *brief* explanation if you feel one is necessary. But no long, drawn-out complicated reasons that make it look like you're searching for excuses.

We are so used to doing favors for people and agreeing to requests, that we say "yes" even if doing so doesn't make sense. Next time, don't be so quick to say "yes." Think first. Is the request reasonable? Is it going to interfere with your own work? Is it compatible with your goals? Perhaps you *should* say "yes"—but at least assess the request before agreeing to it.

You may *want* to say yes to some requests—the ones that relate to your personal and professional goals. But you may have to get out of other commitments before you take on new ones. Explain that you couldn't take on that task right now, but you would like to in the future once you free yourself from other obligations. If they need an answer immediately, don't take any chances—say "no." It's easy to change your mind later and say "yes." But look how hard it is to say "no" once you've already committed yourself with a "yes!"

That future commitment could be your downfall, so don't say "yes" to something just because it's in the future. It's easy to get coerced because you don't feel the immediate time pressure. But chances are, when it's time to fulfill those future commitments, you'll be over your head in activities. Only say "yes" if you *know* you will be less busy then, than you are now (which is unlikely). If you have no reason to think you will be any less busy in the future, treat it as though it *were* now, and say "no."

What if your superior asks you to do something? Well, that certainly relates to your goals—if employment is one of them. But if you schedule your tasks properly, you'll never *have* to say "no." Simply show your planning calendar and explain that there's no time now, *unless* he or she would prefer that you juggle priorities, and delay some of the other tasks you have scheduled.

Recognize that you cannot do everything or be all things to all people. Accept those activities which will further your professional and personal goals. Then don't take on any new ones, unless they are more important than those you are already working on. Even then, they should *displace* something, not add to it.

Conclusion

PUTTING THE IDEAS INTO PRACTICE

The various ideas on saving time fall into two major categories: "Mechanical ideas" and "behavioral ideas." The mechanical ideas are those that can be put into practice immediately without the necessity of a behavioral change. In other words, you don't have to form a new habit in order to make them work for you. An example would be changing the location of your telephone from your desk to the credenza behind you. When the phone rings you have to turn around to pick it up, which means you'll be facing the wall, with your back to the doorway. Since you will avoid eye contact, most people won't try to talk to you while you're on the phone. This idea will work immediately, since you don't have to form the habit of turning around—you have to turn around in order to pick up the phone.

Behavioral ideas are those that require effort on your part in order to make them work. You actually have to form a new habit, changing your behavior in the process. This could take weeks of persistence. For example, if you are currently in the habit of talking on the phone without making notes, a behavioral idea that could save time would be to start recording all calls in a systematic way. This ensures that nothing is forgotten, reduces follow-up calls, increases concentration, and so on. But you have to form the new habit before you can reap the rewards of the idea.

Mechanical ideas are plentiful, and since they require no behavior change, any number of them could be put into practice simultaneously. Although the time saved by each idea may be minimal, collectively they add up to hours. Behavioral ideas, on the other hand, would be overwhelming if you introduced more than one or two at a time. They take several weeks before they become habitual. But the pay back, in terms of time saved, is usually much greater than the same number of mechanical ideas.

To form a new habit you must first become aware of your current behavior and then persistently act out the new behavior you want to acquire until it becomes the new behavior. To give you an idea of time involved, Maxwell Maltz, author of *Psychocybernetics*, claimed it would take 21 days to form a habit. Because the forming of habits is a gradual process, getting organized is a long-term process that could take months or even years.

Since small successes are motivational I suggest you start with a series of mechanical ideas. Clean up your work area, get rid of superfluous material, move your in-basket off your desk, make up a follow-up file, and arrange your materials so they're close at hand. Then choose a behavioral idea that would eliminate a time waster that you're experiencing. For example, if papers tend to accumulate on your desk and you waste time shuffling papers, build the habit of scheduling paperwork in the follow-up file for later action. If you are forever interrupting yourself and others as questions pop into your mind, start using a "Delegation Record" or "Communications Record" to accumulate those questions. If you're putting off important tasks because you don't have time, break the tasks into smaller chunks and schedule them in your planner to work on at specific times.

Each time a behavioral idea has been fully mastered, pick another one and work on it until it, too, has been incorporated into your daily routine.

Most behavioral ideas have a mechanical component as well. For example, making up a follow-up file is mechanical; but using it consistently the way it should be used is behavioral. Similarly, purchasing or making up your own "Organizer" is mechanical, but consistently recording telephone calls in it is behavioral.

Mechanical ideas may have behavioral components as well, but minor ones or they would be classified as behavioral ideas. For example, although using a portable 3-hole punch, hand photocopier or pocket recorder is behavioral, it's hardly a deterrent when you need to punch a document, or copy a paragraph from something you don't want to forget. By comparison, try not to worry or not to procrastinate simply because you need to stop doing these things!

Not recognizing that there are two types of ideas could cause frustration on the part of individuals attempting to put them into practice. Many people give up after a few days, either blaming the ideas or themselves, if they fail to work. But, in fact, the ideas that don't work are usually the "behavioral" ones that will take time to incorporate into their workday.

Don't be discouraged if you fail in your first attempts to put behavioral ideas into practice. And don't lay a guilt trip on yourself. Persistence pays off. You cannot get organized overnight. Work at it gradually. If something simply won't work, regardless of how hard you try, so be it. There are plenty of other ideas that will work. Remember you are a unique individual with a unique personality, management style and thought process. Every idea that works for other people will not necessarily work for you.

The ideas contained in this book and others are summarized in the following **Time Management Checklist**. Incorporate the relevant ideas into your professional and personal life during the months ahead. Getting organized is a rewarding experience. It makes time for the important things in life.

Time
Management
Checklist

The following time tips are categorized under major headings, arranged alphabetically. Simply flip to the area of interest and check off those ideas that you feel will work for you. Then put them into practice. Those requiring no behavioral change on your part will work immediately. Others must be worked on consistently over an extended period of time (3 to 5 weeks) until they become habits.

An idea "does not apply" if it is impossible to implement in your particular situation, or, if you do not think the idea will work for you. Only if you are committed to an idea will it work.

If you are already using a similar idea, great; it affirms that you are managing yourself effectively with reference to time.

Timesaving Ideas	I Do This Now	Does Not Apply	I'll Try This
Business Cards			
1. If your title is not self-explanatory, let your business card explain what you do so it will communicate more effectively.			
2. If you include your fax number on your business cards and letterhead, have the telephone number printed in bold face so people won't dial your fax number by mistake.			
3. Don't have your home telephone number printed on your business cards. This will limit calls to your home and you will make people feel special if you write it onto your card just before handing it to them.			
4. If your name is difficult to pronounce, include a phonetic pronunciation in parenthesis on your business card.			
5. If you keep business cards on file, highlight the telephone numbers for easy reference later.			
Correspondence, Mail			
6. Have your incoming mail diverted to other people for handling except for the 20% or so that must be handled personally.			
7. Have your mail pre-sorted into three folders marked "Important", "Routine" and "Junk Mail." Complete the "Important" first.			
8. Review your mail at a set time each day. Don't grab for it the moment it comes in.			

Timesaving Ideas	I Do This Now	Does Not Apply	I'll Try This
9. If you can't resist grabbing for each piece of incoming mail as it arrives, move the in-basket off your desk, preferably our of sight.			
10. Have your planner in front of you as you review your mail. Record meetings and relevant information in your planner and discard the notice.			
11. Have your mail date-stamped as it is opened.			
12. If you read your junk mail, do it during low energy time, such as just before quitting time.			
13. Have a "To Do" folder for mail that is not important enough to schedule but must be done sometime in the future. Record it on your "To Do" list in your planner.			
14. Eliminate multiple copies of memos, reports, by circulating one copy. Speed up the process with a routing slip saying "It is imperative that this material be circulated promptly. Please read it immediately and place your signature and date opposite your name." You might place your name last for added insurance.			
15. When corresponding, add a postscript to attract attention. Tests show that readers are most likely to read the P.S. and the opening sentence first.			
16. Write brief memos and reports. Outlaw letters over 200 words in length.			

Timesaving Ideas	I Do This Now	Does Not Apply	I'll Try This
17. Have sample letters on hand so you won't have to keep composing new ones for similar situations. Also useful for training others to write letters for you.			
18. If informality is acceptable, jot replies on incoming letters and photocopy for your records if necessary.			
19. Handle each item only once where possible; do it, scrap it, delegate it, or schedule time for it later and put it in your follow-up file.			
20. Highlight key sentences in computer-generated letters so the recipients know they are being contacted by a human, not a machine.			
21. Use headings on your business letters such as "Re: Staff Scheduling" to facilitate filing afterwards.			
22. Don't take the time to write if a brief telephone call will produce the same result.			
23. Address your letters and memos to the one person who should reply or take action. If you address it to two people, each one might leave it to the other.			
24. Use form letters for the routine, repetitive and relatively unimportant correspondence.			
25. When routing correspondence, the last line should indicate its final destination. If the end of the line is the wastebasket, say so.			

Timesaving Ideas	I Do This Now	Does Not Apply	I'll Try This
26. When composing long letters, itemize and number the ideas. This saves time in writing, reading, and replying.			
27. To avoid missing signatures on legal documents, stick "sign here" Post-it Notes at the appropriate spots.			
28. When correcting errors on proofs, mark the words being changed, using a yellow highlighter, so you can quickly verify later that all the changes have been made.			
29. When sending parcels by courier, include a line on the package that reads "In the event of delivery problems, call " (include your name and phone number).			
30. Sign all originals with a colored pen so they can be easily distinguished from the copies.			
31. So requested information won't get "screened out," place a sticker on the envelope: "Contains information requested."			
32. If the secretary types your letters, dictate them as opposed to longhand writing (using dictation equipment).			
33. Don't read routine reports, minutes, letters, etc., after they are typed. Delegate the proofreading to others.			
34. To thin out distribution of reports, don't issue them for several weeks and see who misses them.			

Timesaving Ideas	I Do This Now	Does Not Apply	I'll Try This
35. Work out a system with your secretary to let him or her know the status of paper you have reviewed. For example, initial paper you have seen, circle the initials if you are finished with it, and put an "X" through the initials if it is to be scrapped or recycled.			
36. Make it easy for people to get off the circulation list for routine reports. Every six months ask them to sign and return a form if they want to continue receiving a certain report.			
37. Before throwing paperwork into a "To Do" file for later action, throw away all the excess pages and inserts and keep only what you need (stapled together).			
38. Take advantage of electronic mail, laptop computers, to speed up correspondence.			
39. Reduce paperwork by having reports recorded on cassettes, circulated and subsequently re-corded over.			
40. Stop multiple copies of maga-zines and journals. Subscribe to *one* copy, circulate a copy of the contents page and have staff members indicate which articles they want.			
41. Get off the mailing lists of direct-mail marketing companies if most of the unsolicited material being received is of little value.			
42. Insist on brief letters and re-ports. And encourage people to phone or use electronic mail in-stead of writing.			

Timesaving Ideas	I Do This Now	Does Not Apply	I'll Try This
43. Have more stand-up meetings and fewer reports and memos sent to one another.			
44. Make it a project for someone to review the school's forms and routine reports with a view to eliminating some and combining others.			
45. Keep all paperwork out of sight except for those items you are working on at the time. Otherwise it's distracting.			
46. Make only those copies that are absolutely necessary. Don't waste other people's time by sending them copies of letters they don't need.			
47. When keeping supplies of forms in manila folders, glue a sample to the outside of the file folder for easy identification.			
48. When having correspondence or reports typed by someone else, indicate their urgency by noting the date required. Never use "Rush" or "ASAP."			
49. When editing copy, use a different color so the markings will stand out.			
50. Take the initiative. Use the "unless I hear from you" approach, rather than waiting weeks for a reply to your memos.			
51. When sending correspondence internally, use colored envelopes to signal priority items.			
52. Resist writing when a briefer alternative is possible, such as a telephone call or electronic message.			

Timesaving Ideas	I Do This Now	Does Not Apply	I'll Try This
53. Use self-inking stamps to speed up correspondence. For example, "REMINDER. Your reply to this letter has not yet been received. Please re-read this copy and get back to us."			
54. When circulating paperwork, always highlight the areas that you wish to draw to the recipient's attention.			
Delegation			
55. Whenever you assign a task to a staff member, be sure to (a) get a commitment as to expected completion date, (b) have a follow-up system to ensure commitments are honored and (c) insist that any revisions to the due date are advised *in advance*, not on or after the due date.			
56. Keep a delegation record, or an assignment record, such as the one at the back of the *Taylor Time Planner* to keep track of the delegated tasks.			
57. Schedule time in your planner each week to train staff to take over tasks which you are currently handling.			
58. Don't allow upward delegation. Ask for solutions, not problems.			
59. For complex recurring tasks, delegate a portion of it at a time. Don't overwhelm a person with too much at once.			
60. Set the "due date" ahead of the actual date that you need as "a cushion." But be realistic.			

Timesaving Ideas	I Do This Now	Does Not Apply	I'll Try This
61. Develop written procedures for all repetitive tasks so others can do them with a minimum of training. Involve staff members in writing these procedures.			
62. Let staff members participate in setting their own deadlines on major assignments.			
63. Record in the follow-up sections of your time planner the brief assignments that are due on those days. Use a colored pen to differentiate them from things *you* have to do.			
64. Insist on completed work, not outlines.			
65. Focus on results, not methods. Give advice without interfering.			
66. Don't dole out all the assignments to your most capable people. Give the weaker ones an opportunity to grow.			
67. Delegate meaningful and challenging tasks as well as the simple, boring ones.			
68. Don't keep interrupting with trivial assignments. Accumulate the materials in a folder and review the contents with your delegatee once per day or week.			
69. Don't be a perfectionist; accept jobs that are less than perfect—*unless* the end use warrants perfection.			
70. If you go on an extended conference trip or vacation, spend time briefing your staff members on matters that are likely to occur during your absence.			

Timesaving Ideas	I Do This Now	Does Not Apply	I'll Try This
71. Don't delegate anything you can eliminate. It's a waste of time to have staff members working on unprofitable activities.			
72. Delegate enough authority to your staff members to carry out their responsibilities.			
73. Show trust once you have delegated. Don't waste time looking over shoulders, jumping on every mistake, or interfering needlessly.			
74. Communicate clearly, indicating the details of the assignment, limits of authority, and reporting procedure. Don't rush.			
75. Compliment or reprimand people at the time; don't delay it until performance appraisal time.			
Desk, Working Area			
76. Arrange your office furniture and materials to save time. For example, follow-up file in right-hand drawer, telephone on credenza, bookcase and filing cabinet within reach.			
77. Keep a stack of envelopes near your phone. If someone requests information, address the envelope immediately (while on the phone) to prevent having to retype it later. Photocopy the envelopes if you need the addresses for your records.			
78. If you must have files or reports on your desk, store them in vertical racks rather than in piles.			

Timesaving Ideas	I Do This Now	Does Not Apply	I'll Try This
79. Consider using a stand-up desk to allow you to change position and reduce boredom. (Research shows that standing even improves learning and decision-making.)			
80. Keep your out-basket on your desk to encourage delegation. Have stacking trays, one for each person who reports to you.			
81. Clean out your desk and assign each drawer a specific purpose. Limit yourself to one junk drawer.			
82. Get rid of the pencil caddy that keeps getting knocked over (and usually contains dry pens and worn out pencils). Keep a few spare pens and pencils in your desk drawer instead.			
83. Keep the surface of your desk relatively free from material. Put away paperwork immediately after use.			
84. Locate the telephone behind you, on your credenza, so you are facing the wall instead of people. You will have fewer interruptions while on the telephone.			
Driving Time			
85. Keep a pocket recorder in your car to capture those ideas, things to do that pop into your mind.			
86. Subscribe to monthly cassette tape services, so you can listen to the latest education books while you drive.			

Timesaving Ideas	I Do This Now	Does Not Apply	I'll Try This
87. Carry a "resource kit" in your glove compartment—items you will likely need, such as street map, coins, stapler, tape, safety pins, flashlight. Also a safety kit in your trunk. Include a tire inflator, flares.			
88. Use driving time to plan, rehearse a presentation, evaluate the day's activities—or just to relax if you're uptight.			
Fax Machines			
89. If your fax machine uses thermal paper, make a photocopy of incoming documents before filing or the copy could fade within a few weeks.			
90. If you must have a fax transmittal sheet, simplify it with a minimum of graphics, margins or bold lines and type. They could double the transmission time and long distance costs.			
91. Consider replacing the transmittal pages with Post-it brand fax transmittal memos applied directly to the page being transmitted. It speeds up the process. They can be re-used if sending something else to the same people later.			
92. If you order supplies or books by fax, indicate whether the original will follow to eliminate duplicate orders.			
93. Thermal paper reacts to heat by turning black and obscuring the printing. Don't leave faxes on a heater or window sill exposed to direct sunlight.			

Timesaving Ideas	I Do This Now	Does Not Apply	I'll Try This
94. Keep a list of frequently used fax numbers posted near the machine and have employees add to the list as required.			
95. If it's imperative that someone receive a fax immediately, call them first to alert them. In some companies faxes are so common and abundant that it may not reach them the same day, if ever.			
96. Don't fax dot matrix printing without first photocopying it. Use the largest type possible, with a minimum of 10-point. Avoid typefaces that are hard to read.			
Filing			
97. Use hanging folders to house the manila folders. And don't try to cram too many files into one drawer.			
98. Change the color of the file folders or the tabs each year. Keep current years more accessible.			
99. Don't keep copies of paperwork that are readily available from someone else.			
100. For frequently handled file folders, such as those carried in your briefcase, use plastic ones. For example, Oxford "Ironhide" plastic folders are tearproof, wearproof, and have a non-skid surface.			
101. File according to where you would look for something as opposed to where it should go.			

Timesaving Ideas	I Do This Now	Does Not Apply	I'll Try This
102. To control missing files, require people to sign a "take out" sheet indicating the title of the file being borrowed.			
103. Don't store magazines. Tear out or photocopy the relevant articles and discard or pass along the magazines.			
104. Paste newspaper clippings onto 8½" × 11" 3-hole paper to facilitate filing in 3-ring binders. Photocopy for permanence.			
105. To file small clippings and one-liners, paste them on 3" × 5" index cards and file by category.			
106. File daily. Don't let paperwork pile up. If you do, it becomes an overwhelming task that never gets done.			
107. Never label a file "miscellaneous"; it becomes a tempting dumping ground and makes retrieval more difficult.			
108. Discard as much correspondence and paperwork as possible. If in doubt, throw it out.			
109. Keep frequently used files close at hand in a desk drawer or credenza.			
110. Before tossing paper into the file basket, jot the file name on it while it's fresh in your mind to facilitate filing later.			
111. Allow three or four inches of work space in a drawer. Avoid the necessity of tugging and damaging folders.			

Timesaving Ideas	I Do This Now	Does Not Apply	I'll Try This
112. When finished with a document, even temporarily, don't put it down, put it away.			
113. Try the alphanumerical filing method for quick retrieval.			
114. Don't let everyone keep copies of the same paperwork. Assign one person only to keep past issues of newsletters, minutes, catalogs, etc.			
115. When filing paperwork, record a "throw out date" on it.			
116. Bind "bookstyle" those file copies of newsletters, bulletins, journals, minutes, etc., that must be retained.			
117. Use a follow-up file, coordinated with your planner, to store paperwork relating to scheduled tasks or items to be followed up.			
118. Use 3-ring binders with a clipped logo, masthead, cartoon, etc., for easy identification.			
Goals/Prioritizing			
119. Put your professional and personal goals in writing.			
120. Carry an abbreviated version of your goals with you at all times preferably written into your time planner.			
121. Every week do something that leads you closer to your goals. Schedule time to work on those goal-related activities.			
122. Recognize that you can't do everything. Isolate those activities which will produce the greatest results.			

Timesaving Ideas	I Do This Now	Does Not Apply	I'll Try This
123. Each night, review your objectives for the next day.			
124. Continually ask yourself the question "Is what I am doing now leading me closer to my personal or professional goals?"			
125. Set priorities according to importance, not urgency. Ask yourself "What would be the impact on my job or my life if I didn't do this task?"			
126. Share your goals with others who will be supportive.			
127. Keep the number of goals to a minimum to provide a focus. Perhaps 5 or 6 in any one year.			
128. If a task is not important and not urgent, leave it. If it is not important but is urgent, delegate it. If it is important but not urgent, plan when best to do it. If it is both important and urgent, do it now.			
129. Let each staff member participate in the setting of professional goals. Ownership produces commitment.			
130. Review and revise your goals at least twice a year.			
131. Let your involvement in anything be determined by your goals, not by your availability.			
132. Make sure your goals are measurable, realistic, compatible with one another, and have a deadline.			
133. Set goals in all areas of your life, not just your career or financial status, *e.g.*, family, health, spiritual growth.			

Timesaving Ideas	I Do This Now	Does Not Apply	I'll Try This
134. Develop a personal mission statement first, so your goals will help fulfil your purpose in life.			
135. Involve your family in the personal goal-setting process.			
Home			
136. Get rid of clutter. Photograph bulky items that you have been keeping for nostalgic reasons only. If you haven't used something in over a year, consider getting rid of it.			
137. Do as much shopping as possible by phone or mail.			
138. Double up on tasks, such as cleaning the bathroom while a child is taking a bath.			
139. Have a long extension cord or cordless phone in the kitchen to allow the performance of routine chores while you chat.			
140. Shop in the evening—a time when there are no crowds or line-ups.			
141. Cook dinners in a crockpot so the vegetables and meat cook while you're at work.			
142. Let family members separate their own laundry and let them decide what to wear in the mornings.			
143. Set up a home filing system. Keep one file for income tax receipts. Other files on major categories, such as Family, Bank Accounts, Investments, Legal, Repairs, etc.			

Timesaving Ideas	I Do This Now	Does Not Apply	I'll Try This
144. Keep a stack of birthday cards and thank you notes on hand. Also gifts, if you have children being invited to parties at the last minute.			
145. Use a "job jar" with both pleasant and unpleasant tasks written on slips of paper. Have family members draw one each evening.			
146. Keep a separate "storage" area for spares of frequently used items such as light bulbs, fuses, paper towels, etc. Keep a minimum inventory to eliminate special trips to stores.			
147. Plan meals a week ahead of time and include the necessary items on your shopping list.			
148. To simplify bed making, pull up the sheets and covers *before* you get out of bed. This saves a lot of time running from one side of the bed to the other to get everything lined up.			
149. Wash the bathtub ring while you are still in the tub. Rinse it the minute the water is out. It's easier working from the inside.			
150. Wash pans the moment they leave the stove, before the food sticks. Let them drip dry on the rack while you continue cooking.			
151. Rinse dishes and put in dishwasher directly from the table to avoid dried—on food.			
152. Clean around the sink while you brush your teeth or wash up, or when doing the dishes.			

Timesaving Ideas	I Do This Now	Does Not Apply	I'll Try This
153. Keep a TV or radio in the bathroom or kitchen to catch up on the news while preparing for the day ahead. Buy a radio that is safe for the bathroom.			
154. Consolidate activities such as preparing several meals at once, returning telephone calls at one time, accumulating errands.			
155. Plan ahead. Each evening get out everything you will need in the morning.			
156. Have an office in your home where you write, pay bills, budget and file important papers.			
157. Always have the season's clothes dry-cleaned before you store them.			
158. Make up casseroles in double quantities and freeze them.			
159. Use plastic coat hangers; the wire ones get tangled.			
160. Use cup hooks, picture hangers, etc., to hang necklaces, chains at side of closet.			
161. Store jewelry in separated cases so it doesn't tangle, or use topless egg cartons inside the dresser drawer.			
162. Keep a styrofoam picnic chest in the trunk of your car to store frozen foods while shopping.			
163. Keep a separate set of cleaning supplies in each bathroom.			
164. Attach a heavy extension cord to your vacuum cleaner so you don't have to continually change outlets.			

Timesaving Ideas	I Do This Now	Does Not Apply	I'll Try This
165. When cleaning house, tackle those important, high-traffic areas first.			
166. Put TV trays next to the refrigerator when cleaning it (to hold the contents).			
167. If you have different sized sheets, buy them in different colors or distinctive patterns for easy sorting.			
168. Wash sheets and return to same bed, rather than wash, fold and put away.			
169. Use plastic discs to keep socks together through the washing and drying process.			
170. Organize kitchen cupboards so frequently used items are close to the work area.			
171. Record the whole year's schedule of meetings, children's events, special activities, etc., into your planning calendar.			
172. Maintain a family message center. And a perpetual shopping list.			
173. Plan in advance what you will watch on TV. It can be a time robber.			
174. Use transparent containers for leftovers so you can see what you have in the refrigerator.			
175. Throw out those part bottles of sprays, medicines, etc., which you are afraid to use.			
176. Have more keys made than you think you'll need.			

Timesaving Ideas	I Do This Now	Does Not Apply	I'll Try This
177. Don't be a slave to your telephone. Take messages during the dinner hour—or ignore it completely.			
178. Put away materials immediately after use. Clean up the mess as it's generated.			
179. Buy postage stamps by mail or phone to save trips to the store.			
180. Photocopy birth certificates, marriage certificates, etc., and keep them in your files.			
181. Make up checklists for recurring activities, such as vacation, trips to the cottage, etc., so nothing will be overlooked.			
182. When storing infrequently used items number the cartons and keep index cards listing the items in the cartons.			
183. Hang jackets/blouses on the high bar and pants/skirts on the lower bar for easy mixing and matching.			
184. Form the habit of taking your planning calendar with you wherever you go—even on vacation. You can record those ports of call, favorite restaurants, hotels, people you meet, etc.			
185. Store empty clothes hangers to one side of the closet and use as required. Don't let them mix with used ones.			
186. Keep knick-knacks to a minimum to facilitate cleaning and dusting.			

Timesaving Ideas	I Do This Now	Does Not Apply	I'll Try This
187. Make the bed when you get up; tidy up the room before you leave it. The "do it now" habit saves time later!			
188. Make extra ice cubes and store them in plastic bags so you won't run out when you have company.			
189. Whenever you change a fuse, mark the fuse box until all fuses are identified. Replace burned out fuses the next time you shop so you always have spares.			
190. Exchange money for more time by farming out household chores, gardening, and home maintenance.			
191. Invest time in reading the instruction manuals for newly acquired appliances and labor-saving devices to maximize their use and prevent breakdowns.			
192. Use your telephone to save waiting time by calling ahead to order take-out foods, videos, or to pick up cleaning.			
193. When cleaning out closets or storage rooms, label three cartons "scrap," "give away," and "keep" for sorting as you go along.			
194. Have dirty laundry baskets for both light and dark clothes so you won't have to separate them later.			

Timesaving Ideas	I Do This Now	Does Not Apply	I'll Try This
195. Remove clothes from the dryer as soon as it stops and hang or fold them to prevent wrinkling. (If you forget, throw a damp towel into the dryer and turn it on for another five minutes.)			
196. If you clip coupons, highlight the expiration date at the time so it can be noted quickly later.			
197. If you keep plastic containers to use for leftovers, mark the tops and bottoms with the same number so you can easily match the container with the correct lid.			
198. Keep a form to record loaned items (date and to whom loaned) and check them off when returned. Record borrowed items as well to avoid embarrassment later.			
199. Make a list before shopping and stick to that list; impulsive shopping wastes time *and* money.			
200. Phone the doctor's office before leaving for your appointment to see whether he/she is on schedule. You could probably utilize the waiting time more profitably at home or school.			
201. Use a bank machine for as many transactions as possible, including withdrawals, bill payments, and transfers.			

Timesaving Ideas	I Do This Now	Does Not Apply	I'll Try This
202. Establish a morning routine that doesn't necessitate retracing your steps. For example, make your bed as soon as you get out of it, clean the bathroom before you leave it, brush your teeth in the main floor bathroom, etc.			
Interruptions			
203. Schedule a "quiet hour" a few times each day when you have your calls and visitors intercepted. Close your door if you have one.			
204. Juggle your working hours to reduce exposure to people, *e.g.*, a late lunch hour, flexible hours, working at home for part of the morning, etc.			
205. Lay out your work area so you aren't facing the door or aisles. Constant eye contact begs for interruption.			
206. If you don't have an office, make your work area as private as possible with screens, bookcases, plants.			
207. When people ask if you're busy, tell the truth, *e.g.*, "Yes, I am under pressure to finish this by noon. What is it?" If it's an emergency, do it. If it can wait, tell them you'll get right on it as soon as you finish your current task. Don't jump from job to job.			
208. Locate your in-basket outside your office so people won't have to interrupt you when making a delivery.			

Timesaving Ideas	I Do This Now	Does Not Apply	I'll Try This
209. Use a vacant office or classroom for an hour or so each day if you cannot get privacy at your own work area.			
210. Agree to stop interrupting each other throughout the day. Have everyone accumulate their questions, assignments, or comments and interrupt only once.			
211. Have folders in which to toss material to be given to the interrupters so the time is utilized.			
212. Use body language to indicate that you're busy—don't be so quick to drop your pen and lean back when people barge in.			
213. Look upon most of the interruptions as being part of your job. Schedule extra time for your projects to allow for them.			
214. If staff members find it necessary to interrupt you frequently, consider scheduling a 5 minute stand-up meeting each morning to answer questions.			
215. Keep a tally sheet on how often the various people interrupt you during a day. Talk to the offenders.			
216. Don't encourage lengthy interruptions by offering coffee or telling them to pull up a chair.			
217. Don't store in your office information that people need to access frequently.			
218. If someone interrupts you continuously, suggest that he/she keep a "Delegation Record" or "Communications Record" to accumulate items.			

Timesaving Ideas	I Do This Now	Does Not Apply	I'll Try This
219. Communicate with your secretary. Let him/her know when you are closing your door, for how long, and how he/she should handle calls and impromptu visitors.			
220. Don't close your door for excessively long periods of time or people will think the only way they can see you is to interrupt you.			
221. Get in the habit of working exclusively on priority tasks during your "quiet hours".			
222. Have as much respect for your own time as you have for others'. Don't feel guilty because you are meeting with yourself.			
223. Respond to messages and make callbacks immediately upon completing your "quiet hour."			
224. If you want to see drop-in visitors, meet them in another room or in the reception area rather than at your desk.			
225. Set time limits on all visitors. For example, "Is a half-hour sufficient, Bob—or should we schedule more time later in the week?"			
Meetings			
226. Try to schedule all faculty meetings that are away from the office either at the beginning or end of the day to avoid breaking up the day.			
227. Hold most meetings in someone else's office or a neutral location so it's easier to leave if you have to.			

Timesaving Ideas	I Do This Now	Does Not Apply	I'll Try This
228. Schedule your own brief meetings late in the day—or just before lunch. You will have a natural ending time.			
229. Keep the group as small as possible. Invite only those who must be there. The smaller the group the easier it is to control—and the sooner you'll be finished.			
230. Send out an agenda well in advance. List the agenda items in order of importance.			
231. Allocate a definite amount of time to each agenda item and keep the meeting on track.			
232. Have reports circulated in advance. Don't waste everyone's time by reading lengthy reports or letters during the meeting.			
233. Don't allow meetings to be interrupted. Have telephone calls and visitors intercepted. Have messages posted outside the room.			
234. Use a "Participant's Action Sheet" to record meeting notes and to help keep other people's meetings on track.			
235. Consider holding breakfast meetings. People are usually at their peak—and able to take action the same day. They also consume less time.			
236. If you use tent cards at meetings, use the back surface to print some guidelines for the participants.			

Timesaving Ideas	I Do This Now	Does Not Apply	I'll Try This
237. Have participants fill out a brief evaluation sheet after each major meeting so you can introduce improvements.			
238. Issue minutes promptly. Don't have deadlines coinciding with the next meeting.			
239. Staple a "Meeting Action Sheet" to the front of the minutes summarizing the decisions, responsibilities and deadlines.			
240. Hold brief stand-up meetings. Not only do they move along faster, research shows that people understand complex facts and make decisions faster while standing.			
241. If a person is consistently late for meetings, assign a task, such as picking up the donuts and coffee. Group pressure might remedy the lateness.			
242. If the meeting is over and you intend to have another one, choose the date and time right then, while everyone is there.			
243. Allow a 5 minute stretch break at least every hour.			
244. Start on time; don't wait for late arrivals and don't summarize progress when they do arrive.			
245. Determine the need. If a meeting is not necessary to accomplish the objective, don't hold one.			
246. Investigate the feasibility of making a conference call to eliminate the necessity of a meeting.			

Timesaving Ideas	I Do This Now	Does Not Apply	I'll Try This
247. Beware of regularly scheduled meetings (*e.g.*, second Tuesday of each month). Call meetings only as required, to solve problems, make decisions, communicate important information, and so on.			
248. Don't be trapped into meeting at lunch. You are not combining the two objectives, you are dragging out meetings.			
249. Be aware of the costs of meetings and make sure everyone else is aware of the cost as well. Twenty teachers earning $20 an hour amounts to $400 an hour.			
250. Don't cram too much into the agenda. Skipping hastily over important items in order to finish on schedule is not a time saver in the long run.			
251. Include on the agenda the objective of the meeting. When the objective is reached, the meeting is over.			
252. Allow time for "unscheduled items" and include these on the agenda, compete with time allotment.			
253. When making up the agenda, explain the items more fully, and record in the form of a question when appropriate, to encourage advance thinking and preparation (*i.e.*, don't record "classroom attire;" instead record the question "Should students be permitted to wear hats to class?")			

Timesaving Ideas	I Do This Now	Does Not Apply	I'll Try This
254. Include a map with the meeting notice if there is any doubt whether everyone knows how to get to the meeting site.			
255. To encourage people to arrive on time, schedule a brief but interesting or provocative item first—one that no one will want to miss.			
256. Tell each participant in advance what he or she is expected to contribute. Give them every opportunity to come prepared.			
257. Use a checklist to ensure adequate facilities and equipment before the meeting starts. Lack of a spare projector bulb or magic markers gone dry can waste everyone's time.			
258. Control the seating arrangement with place cards. Separate adversaries. Keeping them on the same side of the table will reduce eye contact, thereby reducing the opportunities for conflict.			
259. Schedule meetings to start at odd times, such as 9:15 a.m. or 10:45 a.m. Meetings called at even times, such as 9 a.m. or 10 a.m. do not have the ring of urgency to them.			
260. Announce the "rules of the game" before you start the meeting, i.e., that you will be keeping to the agenda, controlling the length of discussion, interrupting those who go off on tangents.			

Timesaving Ideas	I Do This Now	Does Not Apply	I'll Try This
261. Write the objective of the meeting on a flipchart for everyone to see. With the objective in plain view, participants are reminded not to wander off target.			
262. If one person is consistently late, try scheduling his or her presentation first on the agenda as a motivation to arrive on time.			
263. If a few people are always late, consider listing "late arrivals" on the minutes, as well as those present and absent.			
264. If you have a "meeting hog" in the group, confront him or her in advance of the meeting and ask for cooperation in helping to draw out "quieter" members of the group.			
265. If you're the chairperson, be enthusiastic and businesslike. The chairperson sets the tone of the meeting.			
266. Make the meeting as interesting as possible, and prepare well for your part in the presentation.			
267. Avoid sarcasm or personal criticism at all times during the meeting. It causes resentment and stifles participation.			
268. Use the meeting for "praise in public" opportunities, such as recognizing anniversaries with the district, special awards, etc.			
269. When individuals are discussing the topic at hand, don't let more loquacious members interrupt them.			

Timesaving Ideas	I Do This Now	Does Not Apply	I'll Try This
270. Be alert to the group's body language. If there are signs of boredom or frustration, call a 5 minute stretch break.			
271. Use visuals. Writing on a flipchart or blackboard helps people to concentrate, keeps them involved in the meeting, and increases chances of their remembering the material. Overheads are even better.			
272. Stick to the agenda. Don't allow participants to sidetrack the meeting. Don't waste time discussing issues that contribute nothing to the objectives of the meeting.			
273. Don't get hung up on parliamentary procedure, unless, of course, you're a Member of Parliament.			
274. Serve coffee *outside* the room at specific times. Leaving coffee inside encourages continual disruptions during the meeting.			
275. If you must have a luncheon meeting, get the important issues out of the way before the food arrives. Once everyone starts eating, talk comes to a standstill. And after eating, people get sluggish and find it harder to concentrate on the business at hand.			
276. Have someone periodically record the time on a flipchart or blackboard for everyone to see.			
277. Cut off trivia with "I know you'll handle that efficiently, so we won't have to worry about it here."			

Timesaving Ideas	I Do This Now	Does Not Apply	I'll Try This
278. Issue minutes promptly following the meeting while the issues are still fresh on everyone's mind. Have deadlines on all follow-ups. Summarize the meeting on a "Meeting Action Sheet" and staple it on top of the minutes.			
279. Always evaluate the success of meetings. Ask what could be improved the next time. Judge success by the results obtained.			
280. Use the meeting evaluation, and your own observations, to make improvements on future meetings.			
281. Whenever invited to a meeting, ask whether it is necessary for you to be there. You may be on the circulation list as a matter of courtesy. Don't attend unless you have to.			
282. If you must attend, see whether you can attend only that part of the meeting which is of value to you or your school.			
283. Where possible, send a delegate to represent you.			
284. Call to confirm meetings or appointments so you won't waste time waiting or find out that your associate had forgotten the appointment altogether.			
285. Arrive on time, but not too early. You may get trapped into unprofitable side conversations.			
286. When attending a meeting, be prepared. Have all the relevant material gathered together well in advance.			

Timesaving Ideas	I Do This Now	Does Not Apply	I'll Try This
287. Lay out your materials before the meeting starts. Don't spend the meeting digging into your briefcase, searching through files, or borrowing pencils, paper clips or paper.			
288. Keep all relevant paperwork in a 3-ring binder, with dividers to separate minutes, functional areas, procedures, etc. Avoid files of unorganized paperwork.			
289. Never sit next to the superintendent. He/she may respond to those questions actually directed at you.			
290. Treat a meeting as you would a trip away from the school so everything doesn't come to a standstill. Delegate during your absence.			
291. Help keep the chairman on track. Record decisions reached and follow-ups required.			
292. Stay out of side conversations. And don't pass notes, it is distracting to everyone. It's better to interrupt the meeting and get it over with.			
293. When the agenda is finished, don't risk prolonging the session by asking "Is there anything else we should discuss?" Adjourn.			
294. If it's imperative that you leave someone else's meeting early, explain in advance so you don't interrupt the meeting with your explanation.			

Timesaving Ideas	I Do This Now	Does Not Apply	I'll Try This
295. If the meeting is less than two hours in length, don't take a formal break. Take a 1 minute stretch or stand-up break instead.			
296. If you take a coffee break don't say "We'll take a 10 minute break." Specify instead to return at "3:25". People's idea of the length of 10 minutes varies greatly.			
297. When meeting for lunch, ask for the check when you order the food so you won't have to wait for it later.			
298. Take working materials with you. In the event of a delay you can slip into an adjoining room to work on it.			
299. Use speedwriting for taking notes at meetings, seminars. For example, leave out all the vowels as in "Orgng yrslf by sttng gls nd plng prjcts n yr clndr."			
300. Where possible keep numbers low, between 4 and 7 participants for effective decision-making.			
301. Ask yourself what would happen if you didn't hold the meeting.			
302. If the group exceeds 12 people, consider two smaller meetings to increase participation.			
303. Keep meetings short—two hours maximum. Generally the longer the meeting the less effective.			
304. If your days are filled with meetings, consider a schoolwide "no meeting day" each week.			

Timesaving Ideas	I Do This Now	Does Not Apply	I'll Try This
Office			
305. Store materials where they are used rather than in centralized cabinets.			
306. Use "frame strips" instead of thumb tacks for quick changing of notices on bulletin boards.			
307. When ordering material or registering for seminars via mail, staple your business card to the registration or order form. Enlarge it on your photocopier to make it easier to read and keep the original for follow-up.			
308. When flyers, envelopes, brochures, etc., are stored in closed cartons, identify the contents by taping a sample on the outside.			
309. If a your secretary is wasting too much time delivering messages to various people, have a message center at his/her desk and let people pick up their own messages when they go by—unless the message is urgent.			
310. Ensure that there are written procedures for all tasks. Involve staff members in writing these procedures.			
311. Insist that staff members question everything they do. Is it necessary? Can it be eliminated, simplified or combined with another task?			
312. Provide training in time management concepts, techniques. Reward innovative shortcuts.			

Timesaving Ideas	I Do This Now	Does Not Apply	I'll Try This
313. Keep a map of the school area posted near the secretary's phone so a person unfamiliar with the area can be easily given directions to the school.			
Office Equipment, Supplies			
314. When you buy or repair equipment, tape the vendor and/or repair person's business card to the underside of the machine so the name and telephone number is at hand in the event of another breakdown.			
315. Make up a master guidebook for all your office equipment by photocopying all the instruction pamphlets onto 8½" × 11" paper and keeping them in a 3-ring binder for easy reference—without fear of them getting lost or misplaced.			
316. When buying a new piece of equipment, get rid of the one it replaces. Don't keep equipment that is never used.			
317. Locate machines close to the people who use them most frequently. Be careful not to expose anyone to constant interruptions by placing them next to their desk; that person normally becomes unofficial repair person.			
318. To reduce idle time at copiers, fax machines, mailing equipment, etc., post operating instructions at the machines (including instructions on how to cope with the most frequently occurring problems).			

Timesaving Ideas	I Do This Now	Does Not Apply	I'll Try This
319. When buying a machine have the vendor conduct a brief training session for all staff members.			
320. Avoid the mess of a glue stick by using a roll-on adhesive applicator, such as "Dryline" by Gillette, for posting those notes, photos, etc.			
321. Don't waste time constantly borrowing items. Have your own stapler, 3-hole punch, scissors, glue stick, pencil sharpener, etc.			
Personal			
322. Say "No" more often. If you're busy or have made other plans, say so. Have more respect for your own time.			
323. Keep the number of credit cards to a minimum. You will have less chance of losing them, less hassle if you *do* lose them, and fewer bills to pay at the end of the month.			
324. Replace New Year's resolutions with specific, realistic goals, and schedule time in your planner to actually work on them.			
325. Periodically ask others how *your* habits waste *their* time and take corrective action.			
326. Exercise regularly. Not only will you feel better and be healthier, mental quickness and recall will be improved.			
327. Don't work excessively long hours or your performance will drop.			

Timesaving Ideas	I Do This Now	Does Not Apply	I'll Try This
328. Develop personal policy statements to help develop self-discipline and accomplish goals. For example, "I will always get up at 6 a.m.; I will never work on Sunday;" etc. Policies also make decision-making easier.			
329. Keep a photocopy of all valuable (and vulnerable) papers such as driver's license, car insurance, birth certificate, credit cards—the entire contents of your wallet. It will be easier to report and replace lost or stolen papers.			
330. Keep a record of family members' clothing sizes, list of loaned items and other personal information in a section of your "personal organizer."			
331. If you use personalized memo pads, include your telephone number to make it easier for people to reach you when you scribble a note to them.			
332. Keep a notebook or file folder handy as you work so you have a place to immediately record those creative ideas that pop into your mind (an "Idea File").			
333. Try to get the first appointment of the day at the doctor's or dentist's office so you won't be kept waiting. And never go to the bank during the Friday noon hour.			
334. Color code your keys with small plastic rings to avoid having to search for the right key.			

Timesaving Ideas	I Do This Now	Does Not Apply	I'll Try This
335. To prevent people from taking your overcoat by mistake, button the top when hanging it up at restaurants and public places.			
336. Accumulate a personal shopping list so you can pick up the items during the course of a week without making special trips.			
337. Carry a small pad of pre-cut masking tape strips (#320 "Scotch Brand" by 3M) in your pocket or purse for sticking up notices, emergency repairs, etc.			
338. If you feel you are organized and not wasting time, keep a "time log" on yourself for a few weeks to determine areas that could still use refinement.			
339. Don't be a perfectionist. Ask yourself "What would be the impact on my job, family and company if I did no further work on this item?"			
Photocopier			
340. Avoid multiple trips to the copier (or fax) machines by accumulating the items in a folder on your desk.			
341. Reduce the volume of paperwork by copying on both sides of the paper, or by reducing the original to fit on one standard page.			
342. Locate the supplies and equipment normally used in conjunction with copying near the machine, *e.g.*, punch, stapler, folders, collator, etc.			

Timesaving Ideas	I Do This Now	Does Not Apply	I'll Try This
343. When using stacks of photo-copied (or printed) forms, place a Post-it note near the end of the pile, reminding people to make more copies before they're all gone.			
344. When photocopying a lengthy report or article, start with the last page so the original and copy will be in the correct order when finished.			
345. Control the use of the copier by assigning entry codes or audi-trons so everyone is held re-sponsible for the number of copies they produce.			
346. When photocopying material from books, magazines, or newspapers for later reference, write the source and other de-tails on a Post-it note and stick it in the margin. Then the refer-ence information is copied along with the material.			
347. Before circulating brief clippings from newspapers, magazines, enlarge them on the photocopier first to make reading easier.			
348. Place a red self-adhesive dot on the master copy of forms and other papers so they won't get mixed in with copies during du-plication.			
349. Buy pre-punched paper for the copier to eliminate the necessity of 3-hole punching.			

Timesaving Ideas	I Do This Now	Does Not Apply	I'll Try This
350. When photocopying or printing materials, store the originals in plastic sleeves and store in a 3-ring binder so they won't get mixed up with the copies or lost or damaged.			
351. Use different colored stock for easy identification of different topics, notes, notices, sched-ules, etc.			
Planning and Scheduling			
352. Schedule "appointments with yourself" to complete priority work before your planner is filled with other people's priori-ties.			
353. If you want to increase your chances of getting to see a busy person, ask for a 10 minute ap-pointment. Busy people will more likely grant *brief* interviews. But stick to your promise unless you're invited to stay longer.			
354. Schedule more time for tasks than you think it will take. Then you won't over-schedule or con-tinually work under pressure.			
355. Don't over-schedule. Leave blank spaces in your planner to allow for emergencies, or other opportunities.			
356. Decide which kinds of activities will be done at different times of the day. Group similar activi-ties.			
357. Use the same planner for home and office. Schedule time for family activities as well as work-related activities.			

Timesaving Ideas	I Do This Now	Does Not Apply	I'll Try This
358. Record all fixed commitments such as future meetings, conventions, holidays, etc., into your planner. Don't rely on notices or memos to remind you.			
359. Use your "prime time" (when you are most alert and energetic) on important and/or difficult jobs. Don't give it away to others.			
360. Be in control of your own life. Don't let others control you. Don't let others' lack of planning become *your* crisis.			
361. Use colored labels to flag important dates in your planning calendar. Highlight "non-negotiable" time with a yellow highlighter.			
362. Carry a supply of yellow Post-it notes in your time planner to highlight urgent requests that come up.			
363. Record into your planner the time you must leave the school when attending events some distance away.			
364. Always confirm appointments before leaving the home or school. Don't assume the other person will remember.			
365. Coordinate your follow-up file with your time planner, making a notation in your planner every time you place something in your follow-up file.			
366. Have your visitors and telephone calls intercepted at certain times during the day so you can work on your priority tasks.			

Timesaving Ideas	I Do This Now	Does Not Apply	I'll Try This
367. Use your time planner for your "To Do" list. Don't keep scraps of paper.			
368. Make up checklists for recurring activities, such as meetings, conventions, so nothing will be overlooked.			
369. Plan your morning the evening before. Lay out the clothes you will wear; pack your briefcase; gather together the items you will need; etc.			
370. Place deadlines on all tasks that you schedule into your planner.			
371. When scheduling a meeting in your planner, jot the items you want discussed on a Post-it note and stick it in your planner beneath the scheduled block of time. Add items as you think of them.			
372. Schedule your priority tasks early in the week so if they have to be displaced, there's still time left to complete them.			
373. Schedule time in your planner for yourself—time for creativity, relaxation, renewal.			
374. Have one planner only and give a photocopy of the next few weeks to your secretary so he/she is aware of your schedule.			
375. When recording appointments in your planner, include the telephone number of the person you are meeting in case you have to contact the person to change the meeting.			

Timesaving Ideas	I Do This Now	Does Not Apply	I'll Try This
Procrastination			
376. Make minor decisions quickly. Don't waste time if the result of a wrong decision would be negligible.			
377. Set goals. People with specific goals in writing generally have less tendency to procrastinate.			
378. Promise yourself a reward upon completing a distasteful or arduous task (anything from a cup of coffee to a new wardrobe).			
379. Tell somebody else about the job you intend to complete. Sticking your neck out provides a greater commitment.			
380. Do the most difficult tasks during your "prime time" when you are at your peak energy level.			
381. Every time you feel an urge to put something off, remind yourself of the benefits of completing the job.			
382. Recognize that you don't have to complete the entire job at one sitting. Do a little at a time by scheduling appointments with yourself.			
383. If you have a particularly unpleasant task to work on, try tackling it when you're on an emotional high, *i.e.*, after having just succeeded at something else or receiving some particularly elating news.			

Timesaving Ideas	I Do This Now	Does Not Apply	I'll Try This
384. Build up early morning momentum by digging right into that first task before you have a chance to dwell on its unpleasantness.			
385. Remember that you are procrastinating if you work on a trivial task while a more important one remains undone. Prioritize the jobs to be done.			
386. Set deadlines for yourself on all tasks.			
387. Adopt the policy "If it's unpleasant, but has to be done, do it now and get it over with."			
Reading			
388. Read books, literature, by actively searching for significant points or information. Use a highlighter and make marginal notes.			
389. A part pad of Post-it notes stuck to the inside cover of a book makes it easy to mark pages for later copying.			
390. Skim books and articles once you have read them, recording the usable ideas you had marked using a pocket recorder. Or jot the ideas onto 3" × 5" index cards.			
391. Reduce reading time by subscribing to relevant newsletters, or abstracts of best-selling books (e.g., *Executive Book Summaries*).			
392. If you must review many magazines, consider subscribing to *Contents* or have the contents pages of the magazines circulated so you can request only those articles you want to read.			

Timesaving Ideas	I Do This Now	Does Not Apply	I'll Try This
393. Keep a folder containing articles torn or photocopies from magazines so you can read while travelling, in waiting rooms, lobbies, or long lineups.			
394. If you can't catch up on your reading while travelling, waiting, or during idle periods, schedule an hour or so each day for the activity.			
395. After you have read a book, don't return it to the shelf before summarizing ideas highlighted. Most ideas stay in the books and never get acted upon.			
396. Take a speedreading course to develop good reading habits, reduce reading time and improve retention.			
397. Save research time by retaining a clipping service to clip articles in your area of interest.			
398. Ask friends and associates to clip articles, book reviews, etc., in your areas of interest, and do the same for them.			
399. Don't feel you have to keep up to date on everything. Limit the subscriptions to magazines, newsletters, journals, and newspapers.			
400. Every few years, allow your subscriptions to expire. Reinstate only those you miss.			
Telephone			
401. Before you phone anyone ask yourself "Is this call necessary?"			

Timesaving Ideas	I Do This Now	Does Not Apply	I'll Try This
402. Keep odd jobs near the phone so you can work on them during a lengthy but necessary call.			
403. Don't put callers on hold without first asking them. For example, "Would you mind waiting while I look that information up or should I call you back?"			
404. When you're stuck on the phone with a long-winded caller, say "I realize you're busy, Fred, so I'll let you go." It's a rare person who'll admit he's not busy.			
405. Schedule "quiet hours" when calls are intercepted. Don't be too willing to be interrupted by long distance calls or VIP's.			
406. Return calls promptly when your "quiet hour" is over.			
407. Before making a call, jot into your telephone log the points you want to discuss so you won't forget anything.			
408. Make notes while you talk, noting any action required on the right hand side of your notebook or "Telephone & Visitors Log".			
409. If the person you are calling is not there, try to get the information from someone else rather than leave a message to call back.			
410. If you must leave a message for someone to call back, tell them the best time to call you.			

Timesaving Ideas	I Do This Now	Does Not Apply	I'll Try This
411. If someone calls for an appointment, try to settle the issue right then and avoid a time consuming meeting.			
412. Take advantage of time savers, such as electronic mail, voice messaging, fax machines, and call forwarding.			
413. Be polite but businesslike on the phone. Get to the point quickly and avoid excessive socializing. For example, "Hi, Jack, what can I do for you?"			
414. Train people to take detailed messages while you're away from your phone (if they can't handle the call themselves). Have them include name, affiliation, reason for call, telephone number and *when the caller can be reached*.			
415. When you can't have your calls intercepted, try the "buddy" system where a staff member takes your calls for an hour and you return the favor later.			
416. If an outgoing call can wait, jot the information on a "telephone log" and delay it until you have another reason to call that person.			
417. Schedule telephone meetings instead of face-to-face meetings whenever possible.			
418. When your secretary intercepts your calls, have her/him say "I'm sorry, he/she is tied up right now. *Can I help you?*" You shouldn't have to call back with information that someone else could have supplied.			

Timesaving Ideas	I Do This Now	Does Not Apply	I'll Try This
419. An alternative to number 418 is to have your secretary say you're tied up or busy and follow with "Should I interrupt him/her?" They seldom will interrupt unless it's urgent.			
420. If you intend to answer the phone, answer on the first ring if possible. It impresses the caller and saves time.			
421. If a conversation drags out and the caller isn't getting to the point, try asking if you could call them right back. They'll generally tell you quickly what they want rather than be called back.			
422. If you are returning someone's call, tell this to the person answering so you won't be screened out.			
423. When leaving a message for someone you are trying to reach, get the name of the person you are talking to. It gives them a greater incentive to get the message through.			
424. If you need information, make those calls early in the morning to get on that person's "To Do" list for the same day.			
425. When leaving a message on someone's answering machine, state your telephone number *twice* so they won't have to rewind the tape if they fail to jot it down the first time.			

Timesaving Ideas	I Do This Now	Does Not Apply	I'll Try This
426. Whenever you have to look up a number in the telephone directory, highlight or circle it to make it easier to locate next time. After you have looked it up twice, add it to your directory.			
427. Summarize an incoming caller's remarks as soon as you feel the objective of the call has been reached. Then politely say "Goodbye." Don't allow calls to drag out.			
428. If your telephone calls seem to run too long, try making your calls standing up. They tend to be briefer if you don't sit down until you hang up.			
429. If you're greeted by an answering machine when you call someone, be sure to indicate the time of your call. Also, enunciate your name carefully, spelling it out if necessary – and *repeat* your name and telephone number just before hanging up.			
430. Don't get trapped into discussing items at length when you will be meeting that person later, anyway. Simply say "Let's discuss that when we meet."			
431. If you are phoning someone and anticipate a lengthy discussion will be necessary, show respect for their time by asking at the start "Do you have ten minutes right now to. . . ." "I have something to discuss that could take . . .", etc.			

Timesaving Ideas	I Do This Now	Does Not Apply	I'll Try This
432. If you have call-waiting and you are expecting an important call, say so at the outset. Continually excusing yourself to take other incoming calls is disrespectful.			
433. Consider using the fax machine instead of the telephone. The message tends to be briefer, to the point, does not lead to verbal tangents, and does not interrupt the other party. Electronic mail is an alternative.			
434. When many people have to be informed by telephone, use the chain technique where you call two people, they each call two people, etc.			
435. Delegate telephone calls to others whenever possible.			
436. Don't be reluctant to talk to machines. Answering machines, voice messaging, and electronic mailboxes are here to stay. Make use of them.			
437. Ask people you phone regularly the best time to reach them. Record the information in your directory. Give other people the same information about yourself.			
Travel			
438. When travelling, use your business card as a bookmark in case you leave the book on the plane or at the airport or hotel.			
439. Always keep emergency cash somewhere other than in your wallet or purse, *e.g.*, a $100 or $50 bill.			

Timesaving Ideas	I Do This Now	Does Not Apply	I'll Try This
440. Use a carry-on bag or briefcase saddlebag to avoid checked luggage where possible.			
441. Use a #10 envelope, preprinted with expense form, to accumulate your receipts, parking tickets, etc., for expense account use.			
442. Keep a small container of miniature toiletries prepacked and used exclusively for trips.			
443. Save time at the security checkpoint by packing most metal items in your suitcase. Show other metal items to security before placing the bag on the belt.			
444. Keep working material and literature in your briefcase for those unpredictable delays and waiting periods.			
445. Use colored, self-adhesive "dot" labels to identify personal effects such as credit cards.			
446. When changing flights or making inquiries, use the phone to avoid long lineups at the check-in or ticket counters.			
447. Don't pack essential presentation materials into checked luggage. Use a carry-on bag for items (and clothing) you will need for your first meeting in the event of delayed or lost luggage.			
448. Make a list of contents of checked luggage and carry it with you to facilitate retrieval or claim if it goes astray. Even knowing what you lost gives peace of mind.			

Timesaving Ideas	I Do This Now	Does Not Apply	I'll Try This
449. Travel light. But bring a collaps-ible nylon bag with you in the event that you accumulate items during your trip.			
450. Make a copy of your airline ticket for easier replacement if it's lost or stolen.			
451. Take a limo or taxi to the airport so you can dispense with paper-work or reading material en-route and avoid time lost park-ing.			
452. If renting a car at your destina-tion, select one that is located at the airport to avoid lengthy de-lays in being shuttled back and forth.			
453. For longer trips, plan in advance the times you will call the office so your assistant or co-workers can have their ques-tions and information at hand.			
454. Take your planner with you wherever you go—even on vaca-tion—so you can record every-thing from hotel confirmation numbers to restaurants you visit.			
455. If you travel overseas, make copies of your passport pages that bear the passport number and personal information. Carry them with you along with three extra passport photos in case you lose your passport.			
456. Make copies of your credit cards by laying them on the photo-copier about 8 to a page. If the embossed numbers don't come out clearly, rub carbon paper over the cards before copying.			

Timesaving Ideas	I Do This Now	Does Not Apply	I'll Try This
457. Travel early in the day; it will increase your chances of getting on another flight if you miss connections or experience a flight cancellation.			
458. When you travel, leave a copy of your itinerary with your school and home. If you record your hotels, telephone numbers, flights, etc., in your time planner, you need only photocopy the planner page.			
459. Use room service at hotels to avoid coffee shop crowds and free up some extra time.			
460. Consider picking up your mail on the way home after a lengthy trip and taking the next morning off to get caught up.			
461. Avoid peak travel times. Book flights that depart and arrive before or after rush hour traffic.			
462. If someone is meeting you at the airport, have them meet you at the "departure level"—it's usually less congested.			
463. Always call before you leave the school or home to ensure the flight is on time.			
464. If your flight is delayed several hours, look for an alternative flight. Most competing airlines will board you at no additional cost.			
465. Arrive at the airport early. Congested highways and airports, combined with the airlines' tightening of their late arrivals policy, could make you miss your flight.			

Timesaving Ideas	I Do This Now	Does Not Apply	I'll Try This
466. Include a prepaid courier "speed pak" among your emergency items in case you have to send material back to the school.			
467. Flying non-stop will decrease the chance of delays. Don't confuse "nonstop" with "direct" flights.			
468. Question each trip. Will a long distance call suffice?			
469. Keep a separate folder on each person or place you plan to visit. Use it to accumulate items to discuss, relevant paperwork.			
470. Use a travel checklist to make sure you don't forget anything.			
471. If you have a choice, select a hotel near your appointments.			
472. Always keep a few customs declaration forms in your briefcase or carry-on bag. Fill the form out in advance during idle time.			
473. Mark your suitcase and carry-on luggage with colored labels for easy identification.			
474. Use the curbside baggage check-in if available and go directly to the departure gate to avoid lineups at the main check-in counter.			
475. Always have a contingency flight in case you miss connections.			
476. Use a good travel agent to avoid wasting time on the phone checking flight times, costs, etc.			

Timesaving Ideas	I Do This Now	Does Not Apply	I'll Try This
477. Keep a compact cassette player in your briefcase so you can listen to educational tapes while you travel.			
478. If you know well ahead of time that you'll be leaving on a trip, schedule your projects so the important ones are completed before the departure date. Get help if needed.			
479. Keep working papers in a large, self-addressed envelope instead of a folder in case you leave it on the plane, hotel, etc. You'll have a better chance of having it returned.			
480. Consider in-room video check-outs to avoid lines at the desk.			
481. If you must wait for checked luggage, use the time to get your rental car or phone the hotel for transportation.			
482. Let people know ahead of time when you will be leaving so they can have requests attended to *before* you leave.			
483. Inform your secretary about items that are likely to come up during your absence and explain how they should be handled.			
484. Magazines, reports, and other paperwork that are circulated should have your name moved to the bottom of the list so as not to cause a backlog for others.			

Timesaving Ideas	I Do This Now	Does Not Apply	I'll Try This
485. If you have an assistant, ask him/her to handle the routine items, discard irrelevant "junk mail," and respond to letters during your absence.			
486. When advising people of your return date, give the date of the *second* work day so you won't be deluged with calls on the first day back.			
487. When leaving a message on your voice mail, provide someone else's name and number who might be able to help the caller.			
488. If it's a professional trip, call the office at a set time every day to provide answers and give directions to staff members.			
489. If it's an *extended* professional trip, have the most important correspondence (that only *you* can handle) sent to your hotel via overnight courier.			
490. Don't schedule appointments on the first day of your return if at all possible.			
491. When you tackle the paperwork upon your return, close your door and have your calls intercepted. Or leave the school early and work at it from home.			
492. Before leaving on a trip, prepare three lists—things you have to do before you go, things to do when you return, and things other people can do for you while you're gone.			

Timesaving Ideas	I Do This Now	Does Not Apply	I'll Try This
Voice Mail			
493. Record "VM" next to the numbers in your telephone directory if the individuals have voice mail. When phoning ask to be connected to their voice mail so you can leave a message without interrupting the person.			
494. If you're greeted by voice mail or an answering machine when you call someone, enunciate your name carefully, spelling it if necessary. Repeat your name and telephone number just before hanging up. State the time of your call.			
495. Include your fax number with the message to encourage people to fax the information to you as opposed to requesting a callback.			
496. Take the time to review the instructions for voice mail and don't skip the training. Many people do not take advantage of all the time saving features because they don't fully understand the system.			
497. If you are having voice mail installed, advise your frequent callers in advance by a letter explaining the system and giving your extension number.			
498. Keep recorded greetings short.			
499. Include your new extension number on your business cards.			
500. Limit menus to a few options only so as not to overwhelm your callers.			

Timesaving Ideas	I Do This Now	Does Not Apply	I'll Try This
501. Give your callers the option of talking to a human being. And let them know how to get back to the receptionist if their call is misdirected.			
502. Change your greetings frequently. Out-of-date greetings make a bad impression.			
503. Don't let your personal voice message be a dead end. Tell callers who else they can dial for assistance when you're not available.			
504. Don't hide behind your voice mail if you're in your office and not busy working on an important project.			

Index